Christo and Jeanne-Claude

THE WÜRTH MUSEUM COLLECTION

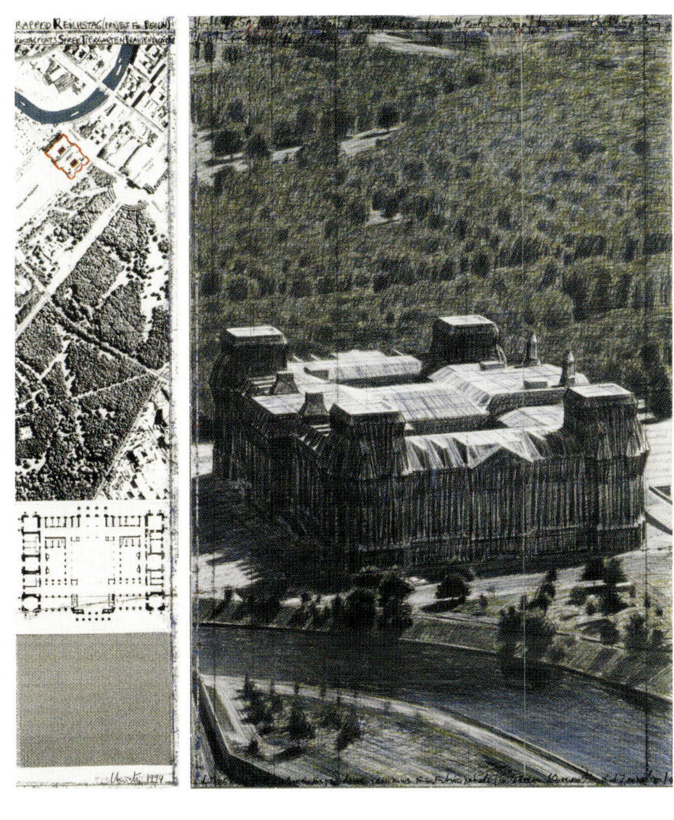

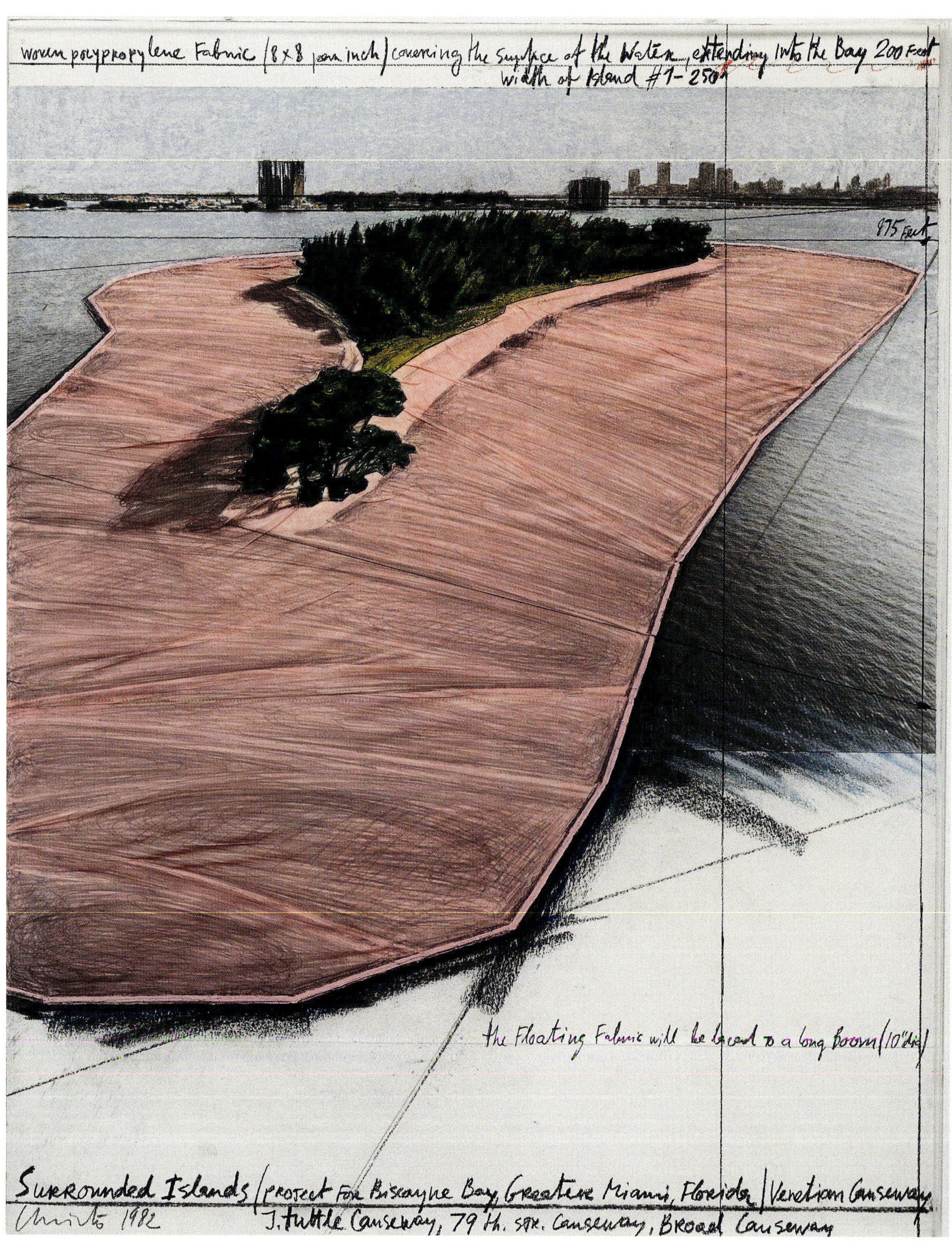

Surrounded Islands, Project for Biscayne Bay, Greater Miami, Florida
Collage, 1982
28 x 22 in.

Christo and Jeanne-Claude

THE WÜRTH MUSEUM COLLECTION

EXHIBITION OFFERED BY THE WÜRTH MUSEUM, KÜNZELSAU, GERMANY
TOUR ORGANIZED BY THE TRUST FOR MUSEUM EXHIBITIONS, WASHINGTON, D.C.

CATALOGUE PRODUCED BY PHILIP WILSON PUBLISHERS, LTD., LONDON,
IN ASSOCIATION WITH THE TRUST FOR MUSEUM EXHIBITIONS

ESSAY, PROF. DR. DIETER RONTE, DIRECTOR, KUNSTMUSEUM BONN, GERMANY
TRANSLATED BY MICHAEL FOSTER
CURATOR, SONJA KLEE, WÜRTH MUSEUM, KÜNZELSAU, GERMANY

Philip Wilson Publishers

Front Cover main image: Drawing for The Gates
Inset Images from left to right: Wrapped Islands, Wrapped Würth Museum; Wrapped Gates; Wrapped Reichstag; Wrapped Umbrellas

Back Cover: Wrapped Trees

Half Title: Wrapped Reichstag, Project for Berlin
Drawing (in two parts), 1994

ISBN 3-89929-049-6 English language hardcover for German speaking countries
ISBN 0 85667 597 0 English language hardcover for rest of the world
ISBN 3-89929-039-9 German language hardcover
ISBN 1 882507-13-4 English language softcover

Edition: 10 9 8 7 6 5 4 3 2 1

Photography Credits:
Wolfgang Volz and others where noted

Designed by Keith Pointing @ Pointing Design Consultancy

Essay translated by Michael Foster

First published by Philip Wilson Publishers Ltd
109 Drysdale Street, The Timber Yard
London N1 6ND
www.philip-wilson.co.uk

Distributed in the United States and Canada by
Palgrave Macmillan, 175 Fifth Avenue, NY 10010

Distributed in Europe and the rest of the world
by I.B. Tauris, 6 Salem Road, London W2 4BU

Printed in Italy by Printer Trento

Works illustrated on pages 43, 75 and 77 are not in this collection.

Contents

Acknowledgments 7

Itinerary 9

Forward by Reinhold Würth 11

Biography of the Artists 14

Essay by Dieter Ronte 22

Catalogue with Project descriptions 45

List of Drawing and Projects 110

Bibliography 125

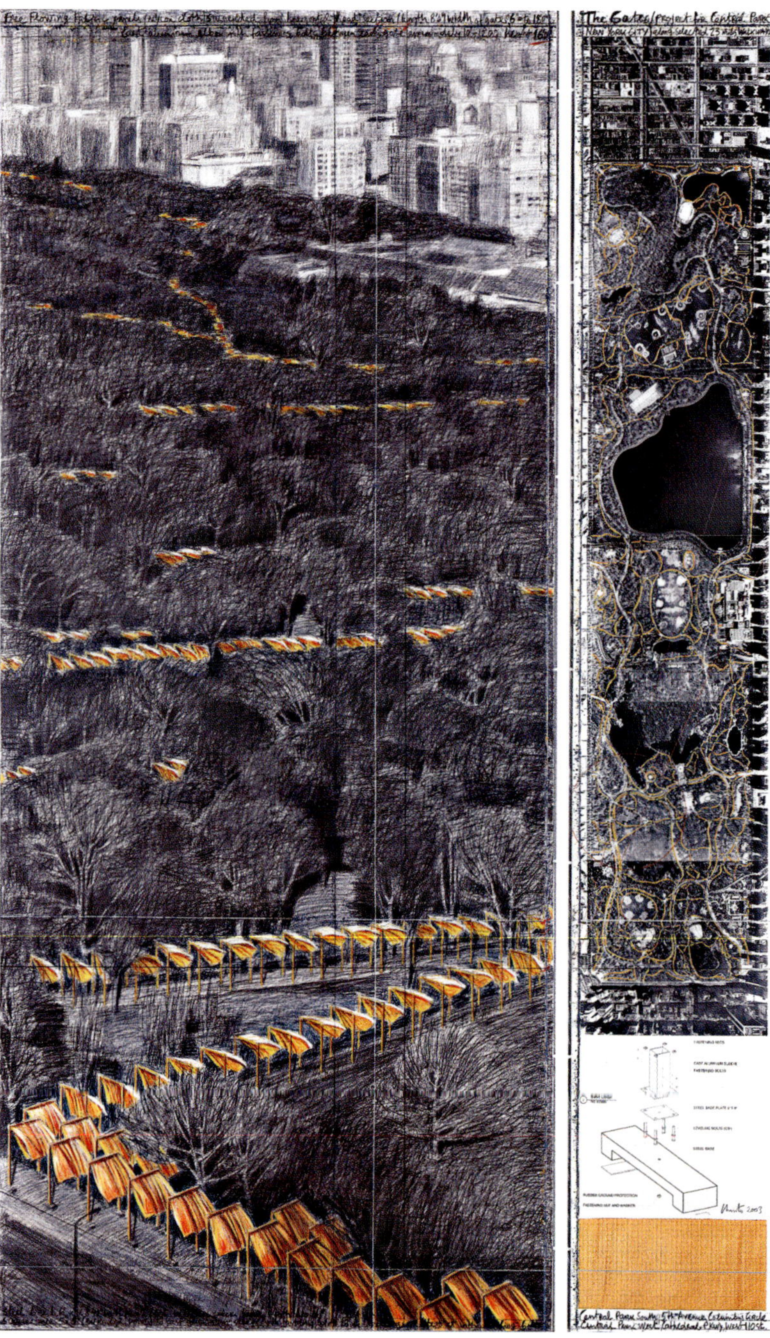

The Gates, Project for Central Park, New York City
Drawing in two parts, 1993
96 x 42 in, 96 x 15 in.

Acknowledgments

This exhibition and catalogue would not be possible without the generosity of the Würth Museum. They deserve a huge thank you for lending us the majority of their comprehensive collection of Christo's works, as well as Reinhold Würth for his support of the project and for having the eye to put together such a collection and the kindness to donate it to the public. This exhibition would never have come to fruition without the help of Sonja Klee, Curator, whose countless e-mails and answers to relentless questions allowed this exhibition to progress.

This exhibition would not have been seen in the United States without the work of the Trust for Museum Exhibitions staff, especially Ginger Crockett, Diane Salisbury, Director of Exhibitions, Elizabeth Old, Exhibitions Coordinator, Christopher Whittington, Registrar, and the rest of the support staff and volunteers.

The spirit of this show would have been seriously lacking if Christo and especially Jeanne-Claude had not been kind enough to be involved. It is a very exciting and busy time for these artists, completing their long awaited *The Gates, Project for Central Park, New York City*; and we are grateful for their collaboration and assistance in making this exhibition possible. Not only was their support of this project necessary, but they generously allowed us to reprint their text from their website about some of their projects.

Thank you also to Philip Wilson Publishers and their staff, especially Philip Wilson, Cangy Venables, and Keith Pointing for the fabulous layout of the catalogue, as well as all their efforts to finish by the deadline.

A very special thanks is due to Professor Dr. Dieter Ronte, Director of the Kunsthalle Bonn, Germany, for writing the essay with little time to spare, and also Michael Foster for his excellent and efficient translation.

And finally a special thank you to those individuals who make it possible for the Trust for Museum Exhibitions to bring such superb exhibitions from all corners of the globe to all areas of the United States: Jack Ring at Barrett (United) Moving & Storage; LeRoy Pettyjohn, Jennifer Schism at Mallory Alexander International Logistics, and Josy Kraft at Josy Kraft ELS AG, Switzerland. Last but not least, we wish to express our gratitude to the U.S. host museums, the National Academy Museum, the Bass Museum of Art, the Portland Museum of Art, the Austin Museum of Art and the Fresno Metropolitan Museum, for their enthusiasm and continuing cooperation. To all who see this exhibition and its catalogue, we say "Enjoy!"

Ann Van Devanter Townsend
Chairman and CEO, Trust for Museum Exhibitions
Washington, D.C.
October, 2004

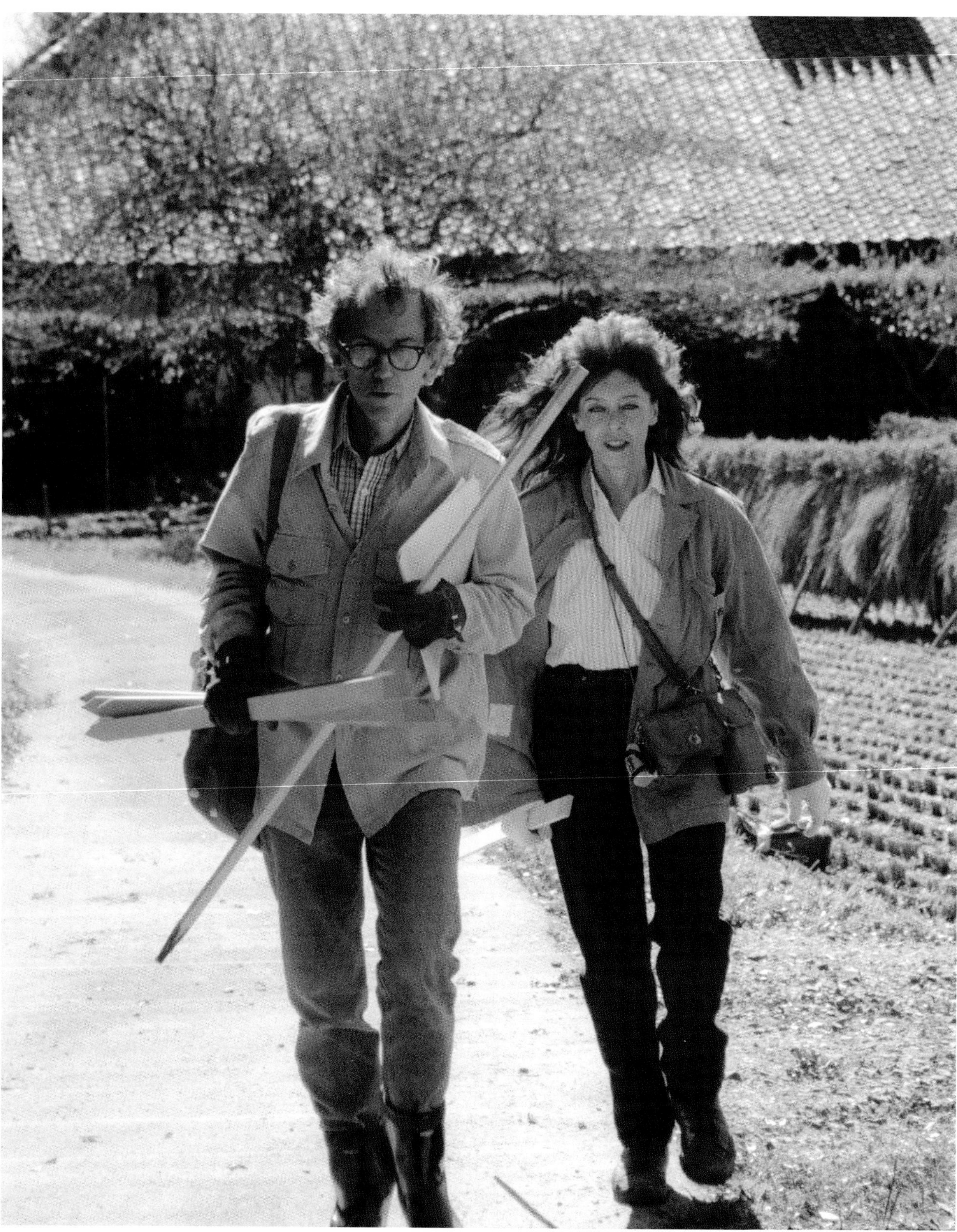

Christo and Jeanne-Claude walking
Photo: Wolfgang Volz

Itinerary

Exhibition Itinerary

National Academy Museum, New York, New York
October 13, 2004 – January 2, 2005

The exhibition at the National Academy Museum is sponsored by:
NURTURE NEW YORK'S NATURE, INC., A NOT-FOR-PROFIT FOUNDATION.
DEUTSCHE BANK
PAUL, HASTINGS, JANOFSKY & WALKER, LLP.

Bass Museum of Art, Miami, Florida
February 11 – April 24, 2005

Portland Museum of Art, Portland, Maine
November 3, 2005 – January 1, 2006

Austin Museum of Art, Austin, Texas
January 28 – April 30, 2006

Fresno Metropolitan Museum, Fresno, California
June 8 – August 20, 2006

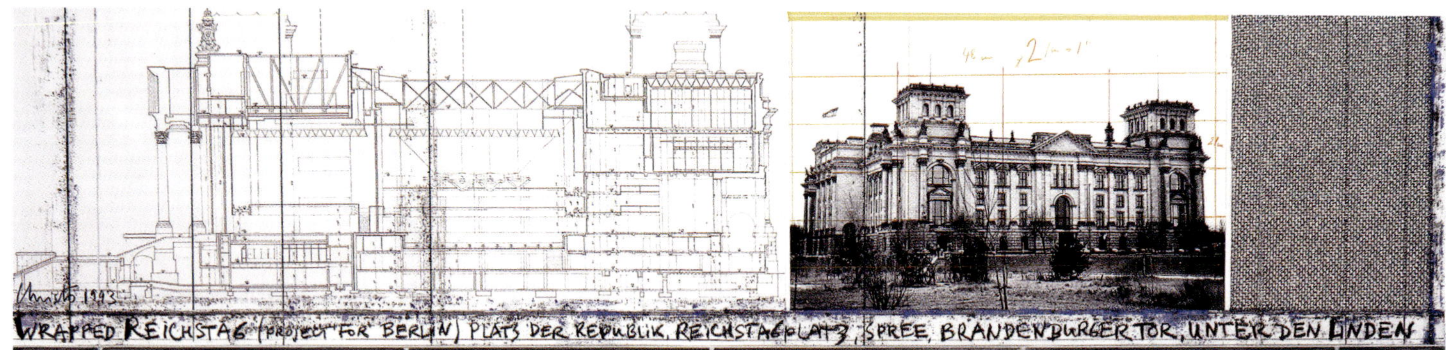

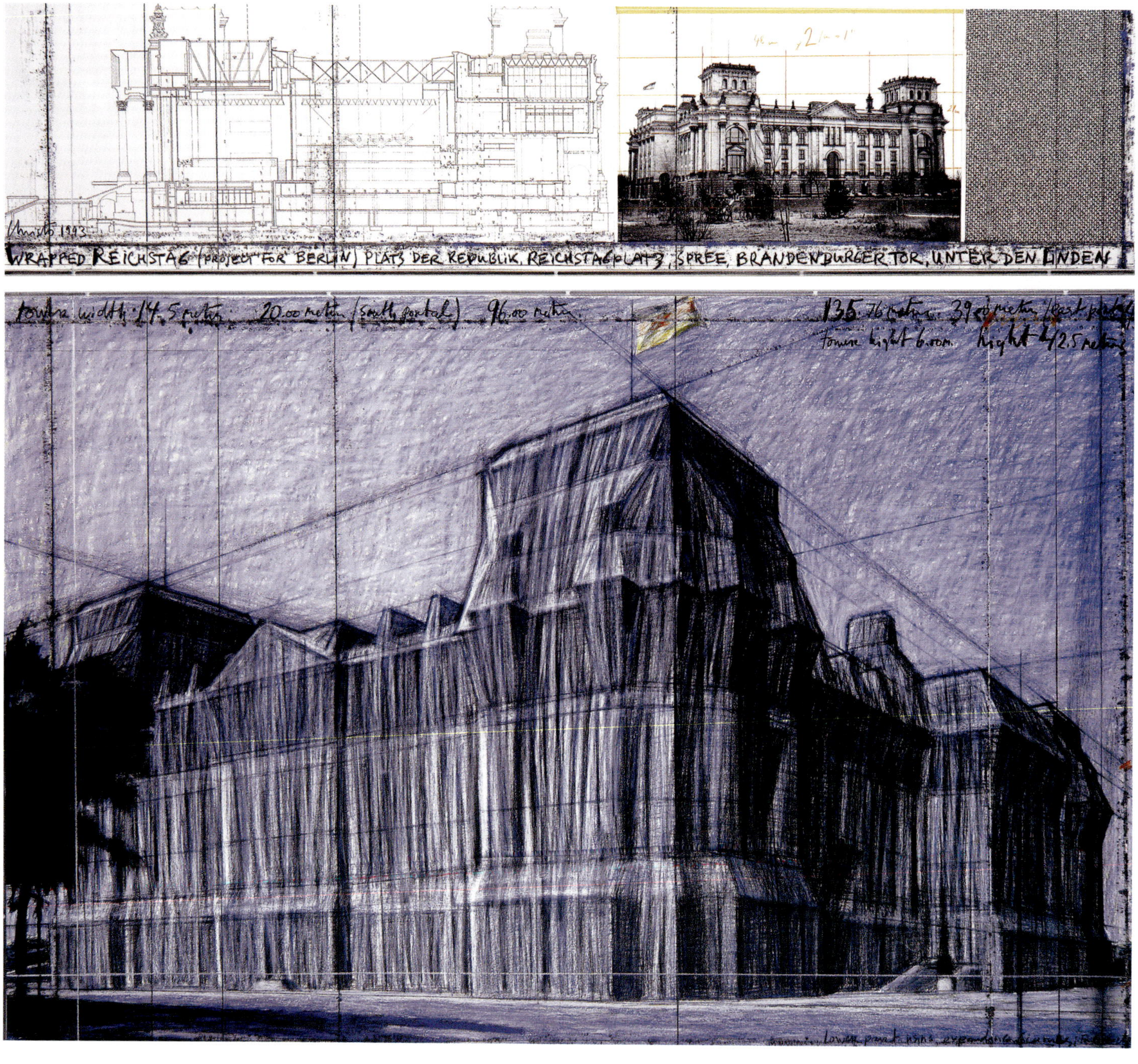

Wrapped Reichstag, Project for Berlin
Drawing (in two parts), 1993
15 x 65 in., 42 x 65 in.

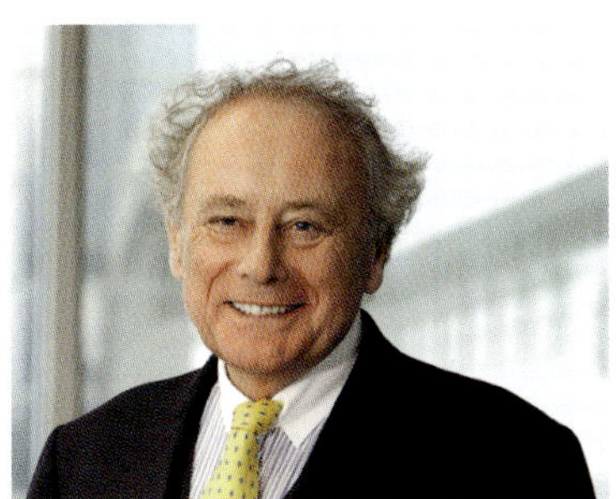

Foreword

Reinhold Würth

Our meeting was one of life's coincidences; Christo and Jeanne-Claude were on their lecture tour of Germany in 1994 and their *Wrapped Reichstag* project was progressing painfully slowly. In the laborious initial stages of the work, with the need for a vote to be taken in the German parliament, the Bundestag, on the wrapping of the venerable Reichstag building, Christo and Jeanne-Claude had to win over the members to vote in favour of the project. One of the efforts made with this aim in mind was an invitation by Christo and Jeanne-Claude to the members of parliament and the decision-makers of the free Hanseatic city of Hamburg to a lecture that my dear wife, Carmen, and I also attended.

I had known Christo and Jeanne-Claude and their work for a number of years; now I made the personal acquaintance of the artists. I found Christo friendly and likeable, and his wife Jeanne-Claude just as charming and eloquent.

Taking up the contact at a first brief meeting in Hamburg we "clicked" immediately. A few weeks before the wrapping of the Reichstag in Berlin, the biggest interior wrapping that Christo and Jeanne-Claude had ever carried out was opened in the Würth Museum, integrated in the new office building of Würth KG in Künzelsau, in the context of the Würth Group's fiftieth anniversary.

This installation attracted an incredible degree of public interest, both in Europe and worldwide.

In the course of our many meetings with Christo and Jeanne-Claude our initial acquaintance gradually grew into a close friendship. I have been greatly enriched by our meetings in Hong Kong, New York and several European cities, both personally and in my understanding of art.

For me, the high point of Christo and Jeanne-Claude's artistic work was without question their wonderful wrapping of the Reichstag building in Berlin. During this time I made the journey to the German capital three times to see this great work of art at different times of day, in different weathers and on different days of the week. The event was a ceaseless popular festival, with picnicking families, newlyweds in their wedding outfits, hippies and students, all intermingling, all friendly, cheerful and at peace in an indescribably joyful atmosphere like some paradise. Very few artists have been able to move an entire nation to the extent that Christo and Jeanne-Claude achieved in 1995 in Berlin.

I have been repeatedly impressed by the artistic ideas of Christo and Jeanne-Claude – ideas that span the whole globe – and that is something that continues to this day, now with their latest project *The Gates in Central Park*. The additional result was the opportunity of incorporating the second largest assembly of Christo's works in Europe into the Würth collection.

Christo and Jeanne-Claude have inspired and enriched the world of art in so many ways. Their artistic creations always have been forward-looking, avant-garde and exemplary for their time. I should like to take the opportunity afforded by this catalogue to congratulate my friends Christo and Jeanne-Claude sincerely once more and to thank them for their friendship.

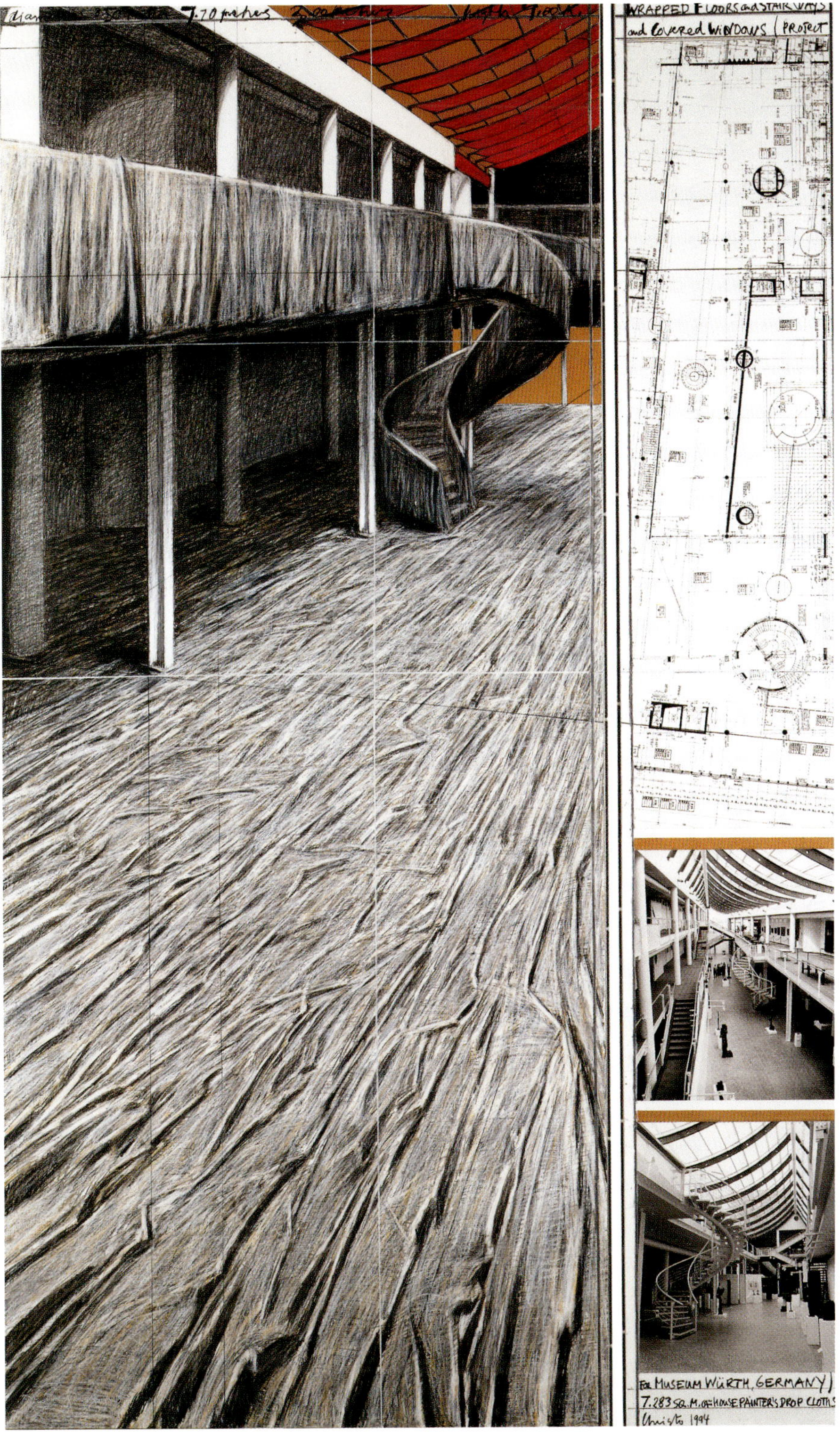

Wrapped Floors and Stairways and Covered Windows, Project for the Museum Würth, Künzelsau, Germany
Collage, in two parts, 1994
30 ½ x 12 in., 30 ½ x 26 ¼ in.

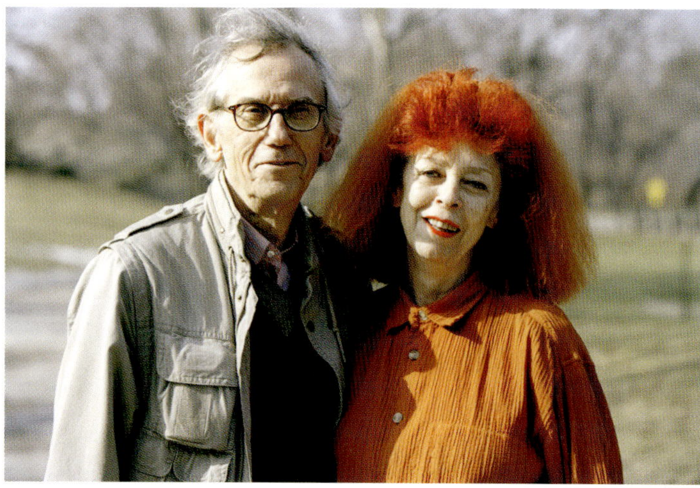

Christo and Jeanne-Claude
Photo: Wolfgang Volz

Biography

1935

Christo: American, born Christo Vladimirov Javacheff, June 13, Gabrovo, of a Bulgarian industrialist family. Jeanne-Claude: American, born Jeanne-Claude Denat de Guillebon, June 13, 1935, Casablanca, of a French military family, educated in France and Switzerland.

1952

Jeanne-Claude. Baccalaureat in Latin and Philosophy, University of Tunis.

1953–1956

Christo: Studies at Fine Arts Academy, Sofia, Bulgaria.

1957

He studies one semester at the Vienna Fine Arts Academy.

1958

Christo arrives in Paris where he meets Jeanne-Claude.

Packages and Wrapped Objects.

1960

Birth of their son, Cyril, May 11. Cyril Christo is a poet. He studied at Cornell University and graduated from Columbia University in 1982. Five books of his poems have been published. In 1998 he married Marie B. Wilkinson.

1961

Project for the Wrapping of a Public Building.

Stacked Oil Barrels, Dockside Packages at Cologne Harbor.

Tarpaulin and rope.

Duration: 2 weeks. Their first collaboration.

1962

Iron Curtain-Wall of Oil Barrels, Rue Visconti, Paris, 1961–1962

240 barrels. Height: 14 ft. Width: 13 ft. Depth: 5 ft 6 in.

Duration: 8 hours.

Stacked Oil Barrels, Gentilly, near Paris.

Wrapped Woman 1962.

Showcases.

1963

Establishment of permanent residence in New York City.

Store Fronts and Show Windows.

1966

Air Package, 1966.
Stedelijk van Abbemuseum, Eindhoven, The Netherlands.
Rubberized canvas balloon and rope Diameter: 17 ft.
Duration: One month.

Wrapped Tree. 1966
42,390 Cubic Feet Package 1966 at the Walker Art Center and the Minneapolis School of Art.
Length: 160 ft. Polyethylene: 8,000 sq ft. Manila rope: 3,000 ft
Duration: Three days.

1968

Wrapped Kunsthalle Berne.
Fabric: 227,000 sq ft
Rope: 10,000 ft.
Duration: 7 days.

Wrapped Fountain and Wrapped Medieval Tower, Spoleto, Italy.
Polyethylene and ropes.
Duration: 3 weeks.

5,600 Cubic meter Package, Documenta 4, Kassel, Germany. 1967–1968
An Air Package 280 ft high, six concrete foundations arranged in a 900 ft diameter circle.
Fabric: 22,000 sq ft, Weight: 14,000 lb. Rope: 12,000 ft.
Duration: Two and a half months.
Corridor Store Front, total area: 1,500 sq ft.
1,240 Oil Barrels Mastaba, and *Two Tons of Stacked Hay.*
Philadelphia Institute of Contemporary Art.

1969

Wrapped Museum of Contemporary Art, Chicago.
Tarpaulin: 10,000 sq ft and rope.
Duration: 40 days.

Wrapped Floor and Stairway. Museum of Contemporary Art, Chicago.
House painter&Mac226;s cotton drop cloths, 2,800 sq ft and rope.
Duration: 40 days.

Wrapped Coast, Little Bay.
One Million Square Feet, Sydney, Australia, Erosion Control fabric: 1,000,000 sq ft and 36 miles (58 km) of ropes.
Duration: Two months.

1970

Wrapped Monuments, Milano: Monument to Vittorio Emanuele, Piazza del Duomo, Milano, Italy.
Polyethylene and rope.
Duration: Two days.

Monument to Leonardo da Vinci, Piazza della Scala, Milano, Italy.
Polyethylene and rope.
Duration: Seven days.

1971

Wrapped Floors, Covered Windows and Wrapped Walk Ways, Haus Lange, Krefeld, Germany.
House painter's cotton drop cloths.
Duration: 30 days.

1972

Valley Curtain, Grand Hogback, Rifle, Colorado, 1970–1972.
Width: 381 & Mac246; 1,250–1,368 ft. Height: 56 &Mac246; 185–365 ft. Nylon polyamide fabric: 142,000 sq ft.
Steel cables: 110,000 lb; 800 tons of concrete.
Duration: 28 hours.

1974

The Wall, Wrapped Roman Wall, Via V. Veneto and Villa, Borghese, Rome, Italy.
Polypropylene fabric and Dacron rope. Height: 49 ft. Length: 820 ft. Width varying between 13 to 18 ft.
Duration: 40 days.

Ocean Front, Newport, Rhode Island.
Surface: 450 x 320 ft. 150,000 sq ft polypropylene fabric floating over the ocean.
Duration: 8 days.

1976

Running Fence, Sonoma and Marin Counties, California, 1972–1976.
18 ft high, 24 ½ miles (39.4 km) long, crossing 14 roads. 2,050 fabric panels: 240,000 sq yds of woven nylon fabric suspended from 90 miles (144 km) of steel cables. 2,080 steel poles, each 3 ½ in. diameter, 21 ft long.
Duration: 14 days.

1977

Mastaba of Abu Dhabi, Project for United Arab Emirates, in progress.

1978

Wrapped Walk Ways, Loose Park, Kansas City, Missouri, 1977–1978. 15,000 sq yds of woven nylon fabric over 2.8 miles (4.5 km) of walkways.
Duration: 14 days.

1979

The Gates, Project for Central Park, New York City, in progress.

1983

Surrounded Islands, Biscayne Bay, Greater Miami, Florida, 1980–1983.
Pink woven polypropylene fabric floating around eleven islands: 6.5 million sq ft.
Duration: 14 days.

1984

Wrapped Floors and Stairways and Covered Windows, Architecture Museum, Basel, Switzerland.
House painter & Mac226;s cotton drop cloths.
Duration: 30 days.

1985

The Pont Neuf Wrapped, Paris, 1975–1985.
4454,178 sq ft woven polyamide fabric. 42,900 ft of rope.
Duration: 14 days.

1991

The Umbrellas, Japan-U.S.A., 1984–1991.
1,340 blue umbrellas in Ibaraki, Japan; 1,760 yellow umbrellas in California. Each umbrella: Height: 19 ft 8 in., Diameter: 28 ft 6 in. Valley size in Japan: Length: 12 miles (19 km). Width: 2.5 miles (4 km). Valley size in USA: Length:18 miles (29 km). Width: 2.5 miles (4 km)
Duration: 18 days.

1992

Over The River, Project for The Arkansas River, Colorado. In progress.

1995

Wrapped Floors and Stairways and Covered Windows. Museum Würth, Künzelsau, Germany, 1995.
House painter&Mac226;s cotton drop cloth on the floor and stairs and brown wrapping paper on the glass of the windows.
Duration: 3 months.

Wrapped Reichstag, Berlin, 1971–1995.
100,000 sq m (1,076,000 sq ft) of polypropylene fabric. 15,600 m (51,181 ft) of rope and 200 metric tons of steel.
Duration: 14 days.

1998

Wrapped Trees, Fondation Beyeler and Berower Park, Riehen-Basel, Switzerland, 1997–1998.
178 trees. 53,283 sq m (592,034 sq ft) of woven polyester fabric, 23 km (14.3 miles) of rope.
Duration: 21 days.

1999

The Wall, 13,000 Oil Barrels, Gasometer, Oberhausen, Germany, 1998–1999.
An indoor installation. Height: 85 ft. Width: 223 ft. Depth: 24 ft.
Duration: 6 months.

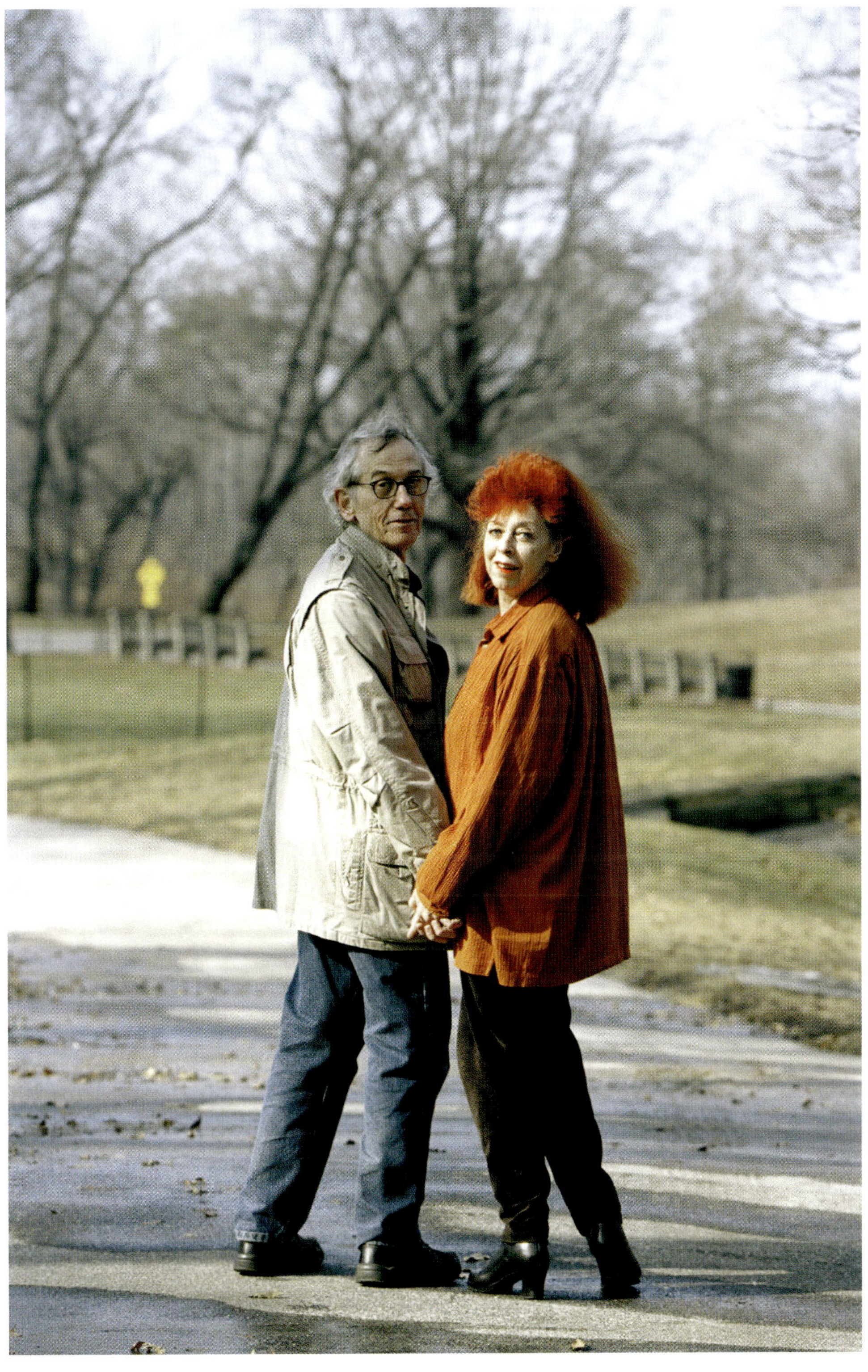

Christo and Jeanne-Claude
Photo: Wolfgang Volz

Christo and Jeanne-Claude

Art generally aims at (re-)presentation, at demonstration; it seeks to clarify things. Christo and Jeanne-Claude achieve the opposite. They obscure objects, buildings, and landscapes by wrapping them. They work in tandem with the things they envelope to give them an aura completely differently from that envisaged by their makers – by the architect of the Reichstag building, for example, or the designer of the Würth company headquarters. The prestigious aspect of such buildings, inside and out, is transformed: it is veiled. Reducing visual accessibility by an increase in obscurity enables the buildings to be perceived in fascinating new ways.

Christo and Jeanne-Claude are true artists nonetheless, because they add something artificial to the buildings without depriving them of their function. The wrapping is temporary; the original aims of the architecture become visible again when the artists withdraw.

Bertold Brecht stated: "The situation becomes so complicated because a simple 'reproduction of reality' can make even less of a statement about reality than ever. A photograph of the Krupp engineering plant or AEG's main factory shows virtually nothing about the organizations that live inside them. The actual reality has slipped away into the functional. The objectification of human relationships, in this case the factory, no longer reveals the latter. It is therefore indeed necessary to 'erect something', something 'artificial' or 'staged'."[1]

This functionalization of givens, this diagonal shift, is precisely the process that Christo and Jeanne-Claude wish to bring about. Their work does not involve concealing things, as is often stated; nor does it consist of uncovering hidden beauty. Instead, it is an act that probes existing things and turns them in on themselves – not to demonstrate their "true" nature or to satisfy any false claims to beauty, but to open up new approaches to them through their changed aspect.

The buildings do not have a "unique character", and they cannot be reduced to a common iconographical denominator. In the deconstructive manner typical of the new constructivism, their content and message varies, along with their degree of beauty or ugliness, significance or insignificance, intactness or disrepair. They start a new life, their history taking an unforeseen turn. Christo and Jeanne-Claude's intervention marks a special moment in the history of a building, a highpoint that will retain its vitality decades after the artists' brief alteration of it has ceased to be visible. This retrospective view, planned in the present for the future, has nothing to do with nostalgia, with fond memories. Rather, it gives the tension inherent in the building a new, wide-ranging dimension that reduces the significance of the many minor things and events associated with the structure, whether positive or negative.

Christo and Jeanne-Claude perceive the things they wrap as partners with a voice of their own, not as lifeless objects or insignificant landscapes. They can be distinctly obstinate participants in an artistic dialogue. The dominance of objects and the fascination they exert on the artists leads to an artistic language of compelling immediacy. Though the grammar of that language is wholly untraditional, its creation is rooted in the status quo, itself the product of tradition. The artists' passage from yesterday to tomorrow, from the status quo to change, takes in drawings, plans, revisions, and photographs (usually by friend and photographer Wolfgang Volz). In this way, the process becomes traceable, revealing an intense preoccupation not only with the object the artists wish to wrap, but also with the prevailing circumstances, which demand working procedures governed by the complex logistics generated by official regulations, political commitments, ecological stipulations, ownership issues, and so on and so forth. The wrapping amounts to an investiture, a rebirth, an inauguration. More than an alteration, it represents complete regeneration for a limited period of time. Wrapping raises the status of an object; it acquires prominence as the embodiment of a new vision achieved by means of a new appearance. The huge physical dimensions of Christo and Jeanne-Claude's projects have resulted in works of art of an unprecedented size.

Christo and Jeanne-Claude have close ties with the Würth Collection. In 1995, they devised *Wrapped Floors and Stairways and Covered Windows: Project for Museum Würth, Künzelsau, Germany,* in which their art formed a second "skin" inside the museum. The semi-diaphanous fabric that they prescribed for the building transformed the interiors and their contents into a series of vague shapes, their outlines not immediately identifiable and thus giving free rein to the imagination. This was achieved without impediment to the use of the building, in which some five hundred people work. Yet the wrapping did require changes to customary working procedures; with familiar things removed from sight, everyday visual experiences were literally displaced, engaging the users' memory, imagination, and curiosity, and encouraging them to make new discoveries.

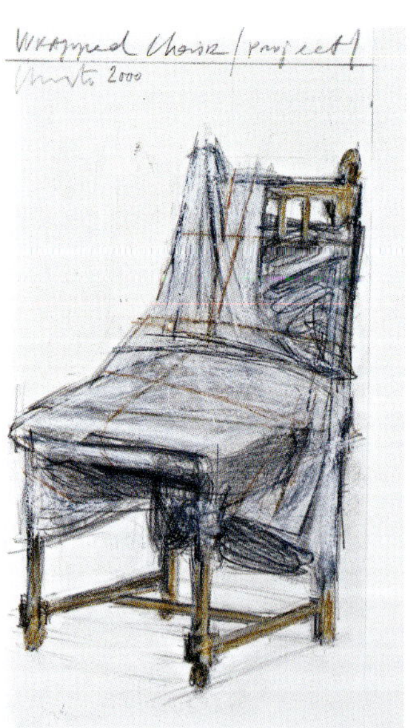

Wrapped Chair (Project)
Drawing, 2000
8 ⅞ x 4 ¾ in.

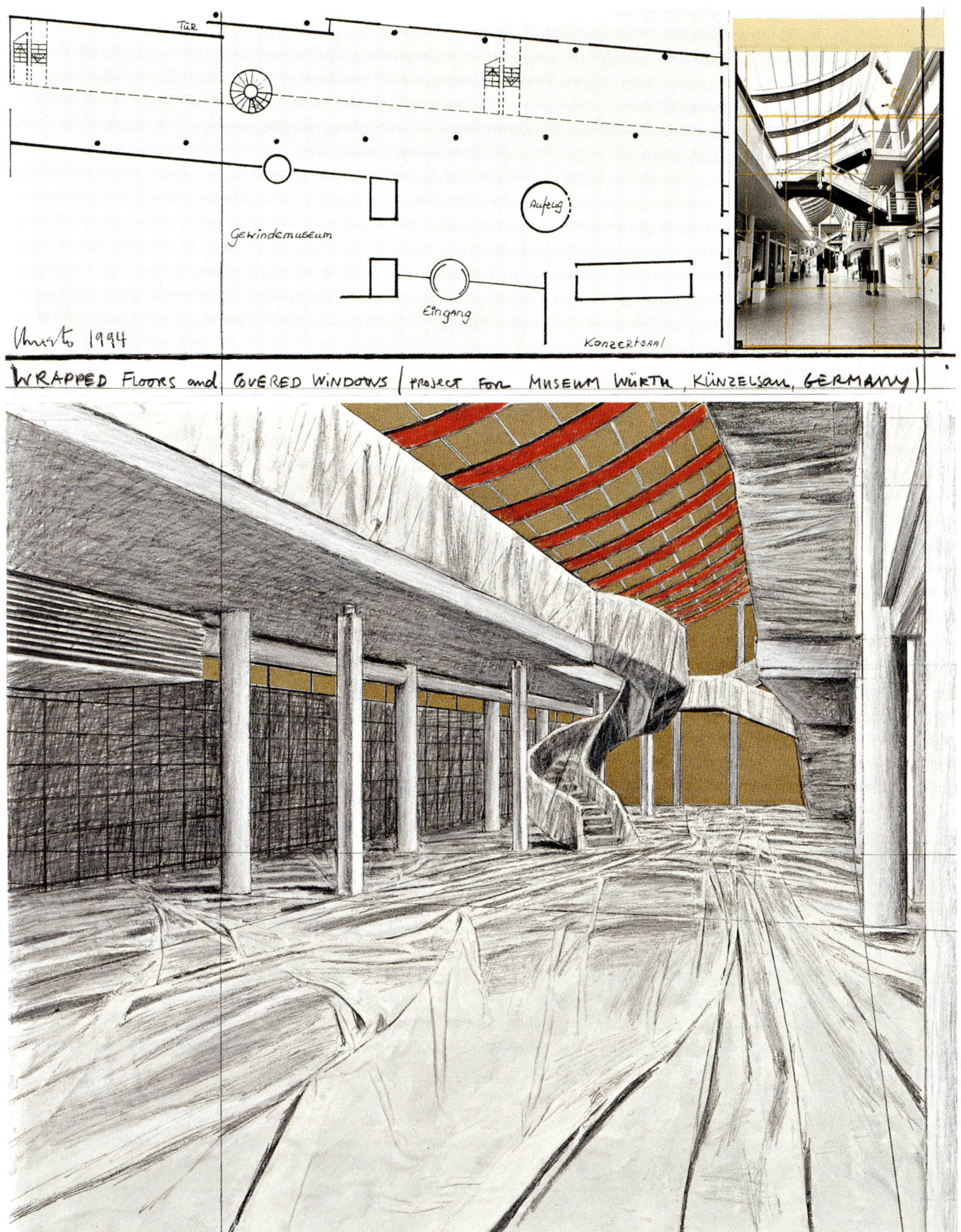

Wrapped Floors and Stairways and Covered Windows, Project for the Museum Würth, Künzelsau, Germany
Collage, in two parts, 1994
12 x 30 ½ in., 26 ¼ x 30 ½ in.

The same applies to Christo's wrapped furniture, *Wrapped Chair, 2002*. No longer usable, the wrapped furniture consistently provokes new perceptions of working procedures and a rethinking of function. This interplay between the unfamiliar and the familiar, between remoteness and closeness, subverts established values, dissolves clichés, and encourages everyone to adopt a standpoint with regard to a work of art, whether favorable or not. At the very least, this approach helps people to understand that art can make a difference in everyday contexts. Conversely, such contexts may grant art new aspects.

Intensely idiosyncratic, Christo and Jeanne-Claude's works are absolutely precise interventions aimed at reordering and reformulating. The artists are not only interested in the beauty of appearances. Instead, they seek truth in the specifics, because their truth exists for only a short time. These artists find truths outside the practical arrangements dictated by functionalist logic.

The Würth Collection contains a representative selection of Christo and Jeanne-Claude's oeuvre. *Wrapped Trees, Fondation Beyeler and Berower Park, Riehen, Switzerland* dates from 1998 and is documented in the collection by several preparatory collages and photographs of the completed project. In this project, which caused a sensation in Switzerland, the artists reinterpreted nature by wrapping 178 trees on the grounds of the Fondation Beyeler and the neighboring field with 600,000 square feet of polyester fabric, tied with 14 miles of rope to give the trees a strikingly individual presence. This was not their first work with trees: Christo created a *Wrapped Tree* in 1968 for the Stedelijk Van Abbemuseum, Eindhoven, and planned *Wrapped Trees* for the garden of the Museum of Modern Art, New York. With the leafless branches pressing into the wrapping, the trees in Riehen became transparent, acquiring a diaphanous character like a piece of Gothic architecture. They came to life at a time of year when trees are leafless and seem barren. The result was a richly orchestrated

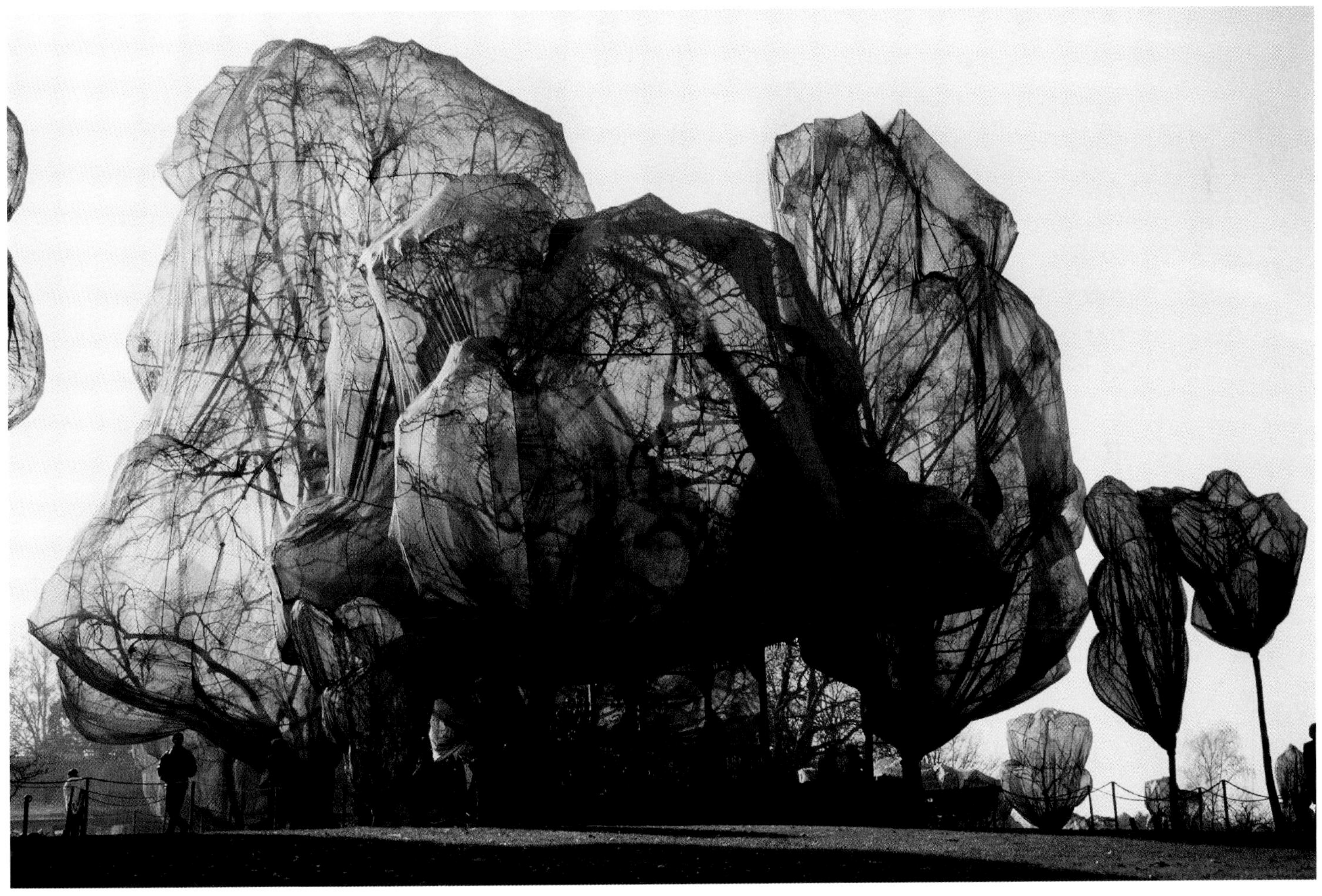

Wrapped Trees, Fondation Beyeler and Berower Park, Riehen, Switzerland, 1997–1998
Photograph
20 ¼ x 28 in.
Photo: Wolfgang Volz

exchange among oaks, ashes, chestnut trees, plum trees, cherry trees, linden trees, ginkgoes, beeches, plane trees, maples, trumpet trees, hazels, and willows.

Most of the artists' earlier projects are represented in the collection, including *Running Fence, Sonoma and Marin Counties, California, 1972–1976, The Pont Neuf Wrapped, 1975–1785, Wrapped Reichstag, Berlin, 1971-1995*; and the indoor installation *The Wall, 13,000 Barrels, Oberhausen, Germany, 1999*. Proceeds from the sale of preparatory works relating to past projects help to fund new ones. Christo and Jeanne-Claude first planned to wrap a public building in 1961, but large-scale projects of this kind often could not be realized, and the artists found it easier to wrap things such as furniture, motorbikes, traffic signs, and cars. These early works established their reputation. Like the Nouveaux Réalistes, they took *objets trouvés* and readymades in the form of industrial wares and discarded consumer goods as the basis of their works. Wrapping, which Man Ray had once experimented with briefly, to create photographs, removed the objects from sight and gave them a new, unexpected poetic aura – the poetry of commonplace industrial and consumer products. The formula espoused by the Nouveaux Réalistes was: object = objective = real = reality. The lie inherent in illusionistic painting was jettisoned in favor a new poetry of reality.

Wrapping public buildings was a more difficult undertaking, as the debate surrounding the Christos' proposed wrapping of the Reichstag building has made only too clear. "Time, money, and officialdom are the only things preventing him from wrapping public buildings such as sports stadiums, town halls, museums, and warehouses, all of which have below-ground entrances that would permit them to carry on functioning. One of Christo and Jeanne-Claude's plans is to wrap a building in Manhattan. It is to be hoped that some institution or other – a foundation or a museum that has remained open-minded – will commission its own building to be wrapped."[2] Such hopes took some time to be fulfilled. They became reality only because Christo and Jeanne-Claude had learned to operate on more than an aesthetic level, developing extraordinary logistical skills that have been responsible for the realization of everything from *Valley Curtain: Project for Rifle, Colorado* (1972) to the *Wrapped Reichstag, Berlin* (1995), from *Wrapped Coast, Little Bay, Australia* (1969) to the work at Riehen in Switzerland. All of these projects required intensive planning and organization, including obtaining permission from local authorities and hiring and supervising hundreds of workers.

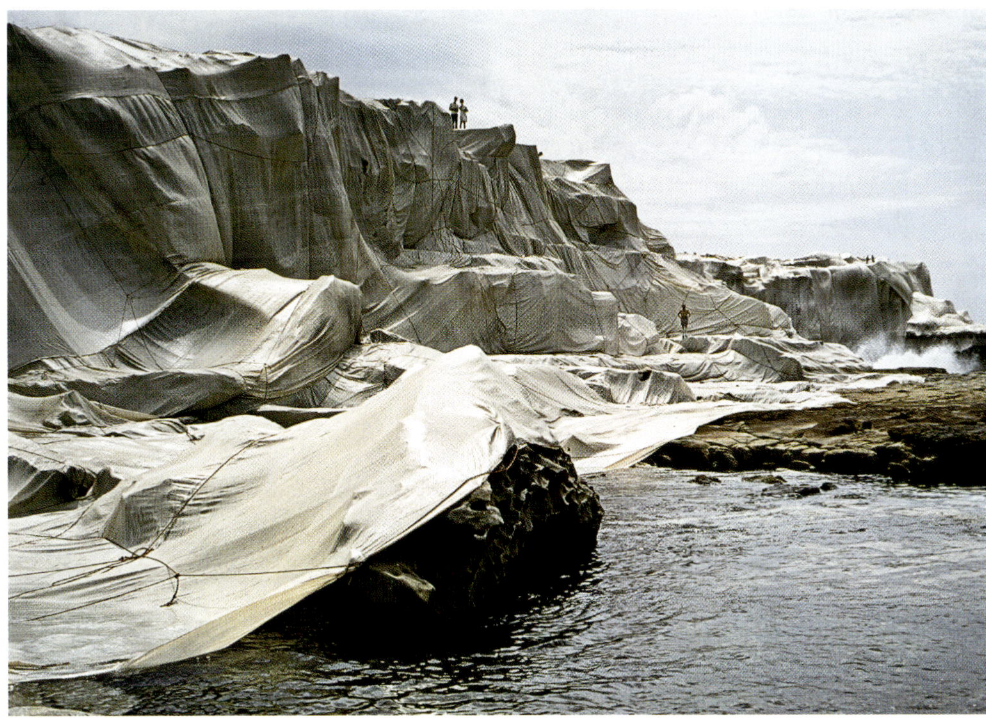

Wrapped Coast, One Million Square Feet, Little Bay, Australia, 1968–1969
Photograph, 1969
28 x 39 ¾ in.
Photo: Harry Shunk

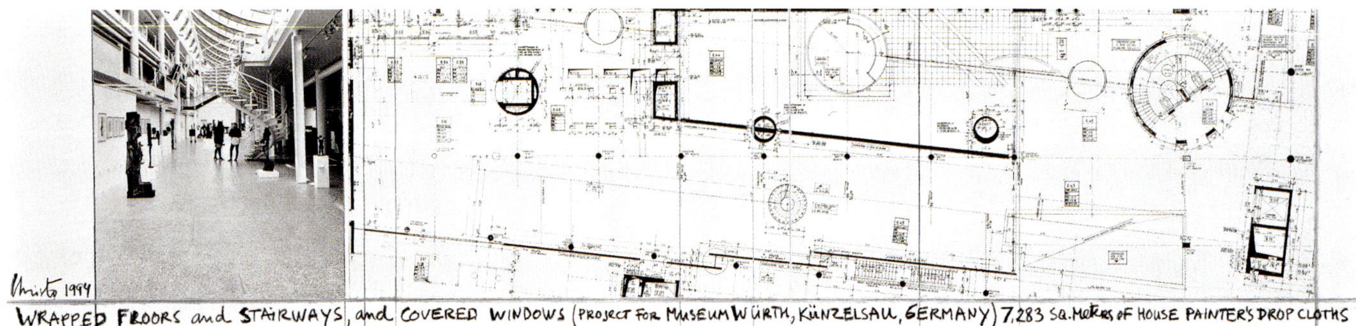

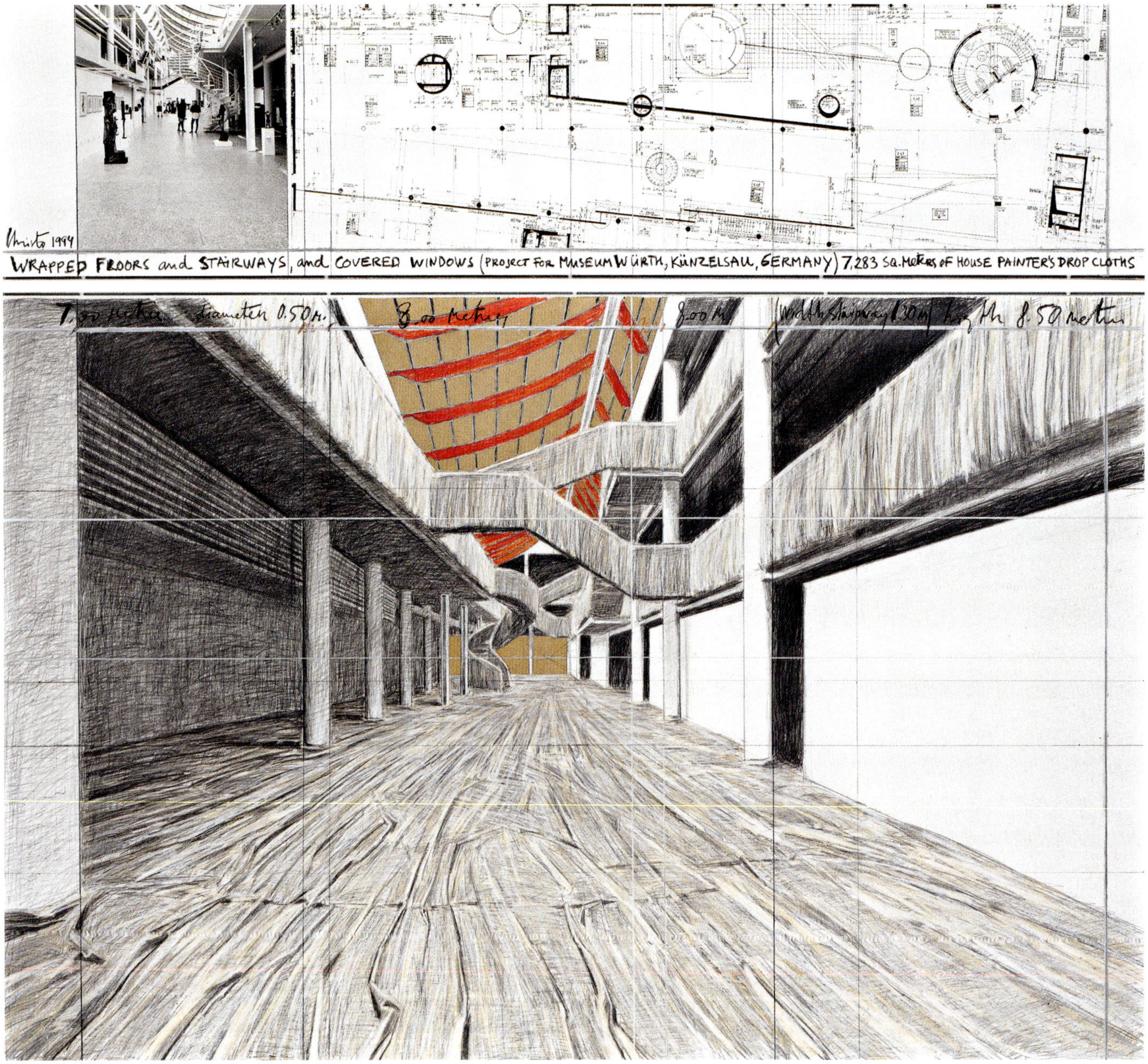

Wrapped Floors and Stairways and Covered Windows, Project for the Museum Würth, Künzelsau, Germany
Drawing (in two parts), 1994
15 x 65 in., 42 x 65 in.

For their major projects the artists have always selected places of special significance. Like Christo and Jeanne-Claude's other large-scale works, the Würth installation was devised so that the building could continue to be used. Designed and constructed by the Stuttgart architects Maja Djordjevie-Müller and Siegfried Müller, the company headquarters was completed in 1991. A total of 30,000 square feet of floor space, in the museum and part of the headquarters, were covered with drop cloths, material used by home decorators in the United States to protect furniture and floors during painting. Twenty-five people, headed by Josy Kraft and Wolfgang Volz, completed the wrapping in time for the company's fiftieth anniversary.

The artists did not subordinate their activity to the building. Neither did they subordinate the building to their activity. They worked in and with the architecture. Irrespective of size, their wrappings, from the early consumer objects and *Covered Windows, Museum Würth*, 1995 to their current projects, have always been marked by a process of give and take in the development of new forms, new lighting, and new outlines, and in the adjustment of diaphanous and transparent qualities. The result has been to transpose the objects onto another plane, to heighten them without putting them on a pedestal in the traditional way. In Künzelsau, Christo and Jeanne-Claude used their experience to transform an ordinary functional building into the locus of an intellectual and aesthetic encounter.

Christo and Jeanne-Claude are both visionaries and realists, both inventors and retracers, both a couple and two independent artists. They devise things, they recognize, envisage, sense, and establish them. The economics of their art is fundamentally idealistic: they use only their own money, financing projects by the sale of their work. They are astonishingly rigorous in this essentially anti-modern approach. They reject sponsorship; they look for buyers, not patrons, because the latter might attempt to influence their work. This means leading relatively modest lives, doing without a car, a country mansion, a yacht, and membership of exclusive riding and golf clubs. More importantly, it means constantly initiating major projects.

They seek to completely fund all of their projects – which costs nothing to visitors – by means of aesthetic recycling, the sale of original works created in connection with their projects. In this way, the financial risk inherent in major projects is borne by the artists, not by the purchasers of their work. This applies, too, to the aesthetic risks. The dominant position of the works of Christo and Jeanne-Claude within the Würth Collection is remarkable in that the major projects to which most of the items relate were temporary and therefore no longer exist. Yet Christo's early preparatory works generated by the projects are so compelling in their presence and individuality that they more than hold their own with other traditional works of art in the collection.

Christo and Jeanne-Claude think three-dimensionally, in terms of reality, not of the illusions conjured up by painting. They use photography as an aid, involving Wolfgang Volz in their work almost as an equal. Their images, illustrations, and objects in the Würth Collection vehemently oppose the illusions of painting. Christo and Jeanne-Claude's works have become irreplaceable factors in the dialogue generated by the existence within the collection of a variety of approaches: they put the case most emphatically for the truth of a vision that is not abstract but founded in the experience of reality.

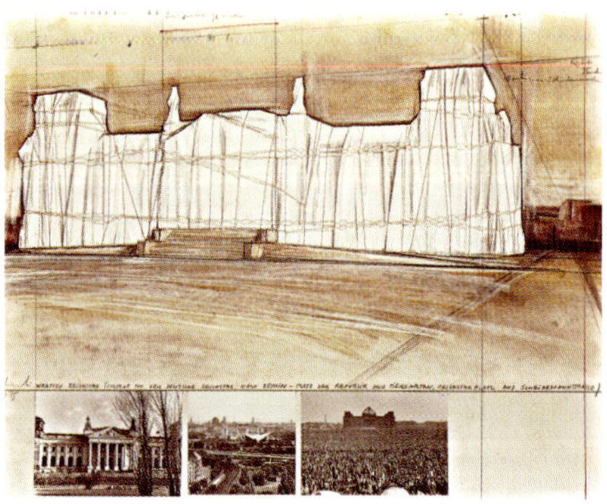

Wrapped Reichstag, Project for Berlin
Collage, 1975
22 x 28 in.

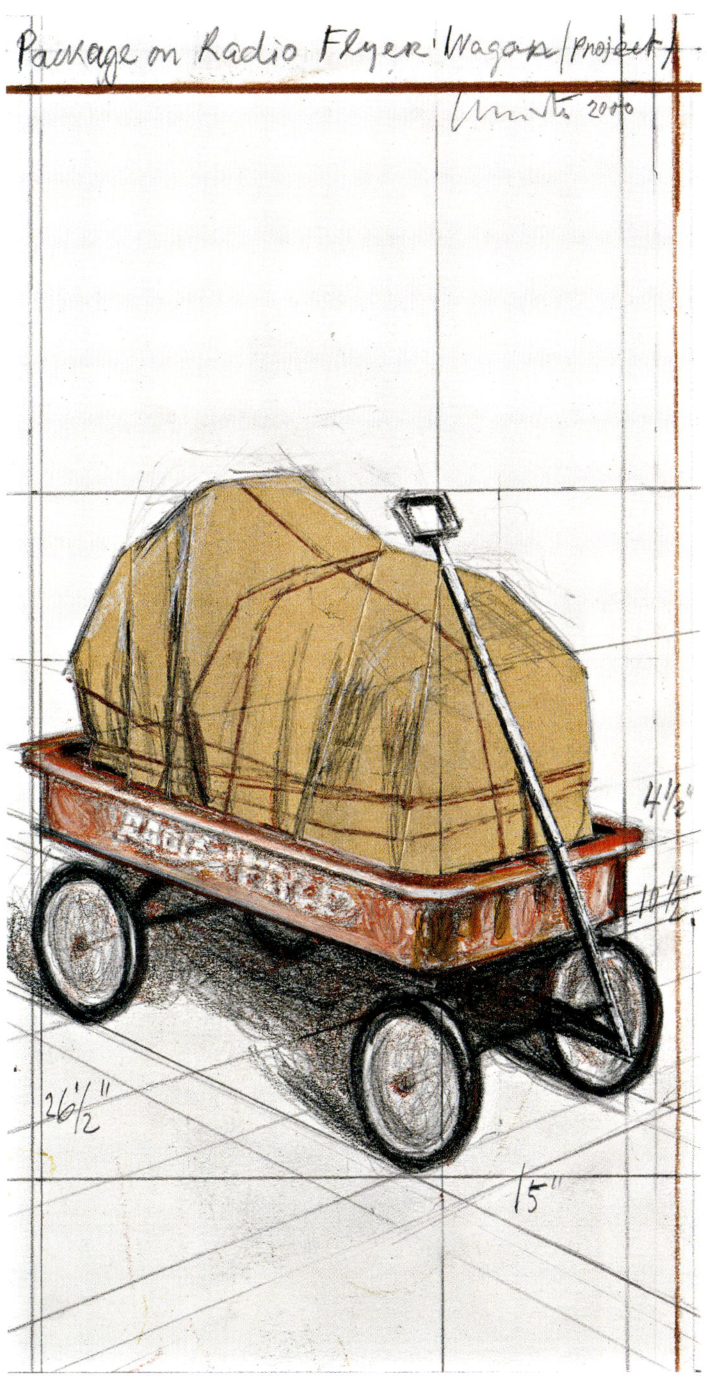

Package on Radio Flyer Wagon (Project)
Collage, 2000
8 ⅞ x 4 ¾ in.

The Würth Collection is quite broad; it does, however, have a certain focus that reflects the preferences of the collector, Reinhold Würth. In Germany the wrapping of the Reichstag building made national figures of the artists, who had helped articulate the wish for a new, modern nation, a Germany that would break with taboos and allow art to invade the political arena. The Reichstag wrapping significantly affected attitudes towards the remodeling of Berlin as the capital of a reunited Germany; it mobilized emotional and cultural reactions to the old Reichstag building in a new context.

Since 2001 the Museum Würth has systematically expanded its Christo collection. The additions include items related to a major new work: *The Gates: Project for Central Park, New York*. The artists plan to set up a series of 7,500 suspended fabric panels that follows the winding network of paths throughout the vast park. *The Gates* pays homage to the park's function as a center of leisure activity, as a place where the city's inhabitants meet, relax, and experience things outside the norm of their urban existence. But the artists also redraw the map, as it were, turning the landscaped area with its famous rock formations into a huge piece of architecture, cultivated and accessible on foot. *The Gates* will also give Christo and Jeanne-Claude the opportunity of honoring a place in which they have felt at home for several decades.

The size of Christo and Jeanne-Claude's project matches that of Central Park. Rather than deterring them, huge physical dimensions have always proved an inspiration to these artists. They enjoy working on a large scale. Their structuring of Central Park offers a contrast to the city skyline, to the architecture that has risen higher and higher, reaching ever further into the sky. Now, after the shock of September 11, 2001, an even taller building is to replace the World Trade Center as a demonstration of national strength and economic power. Christo and Jeanne-Claude counter this with temporary architecture in a landscaped context that will bear witness to the strength and feelings of Central Park's

The Gates, Project for Central Park, New York City
Collage in two parts, 1992
12 x 30 ½ in., 26 ¼ x 30 ½ in.

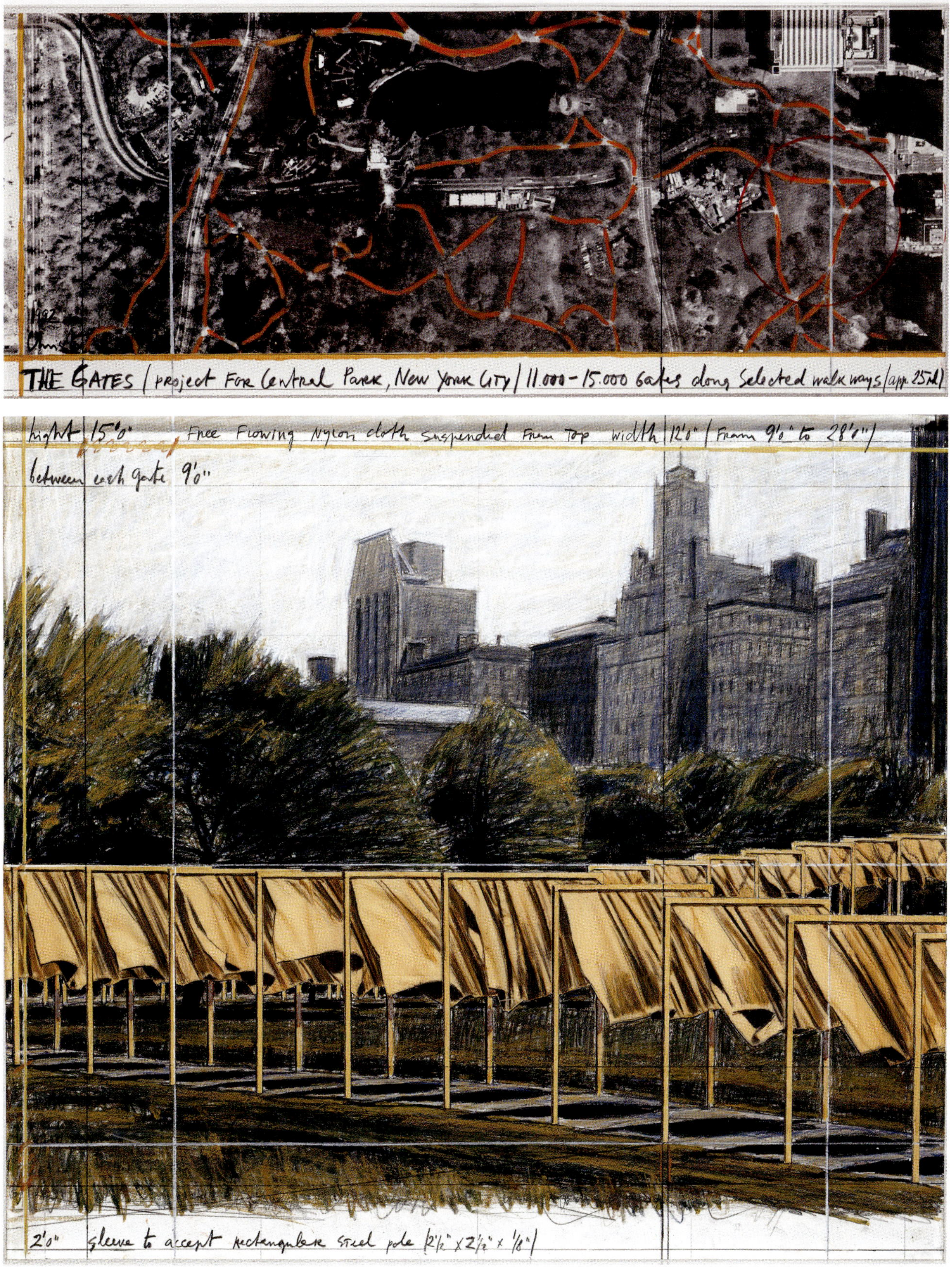

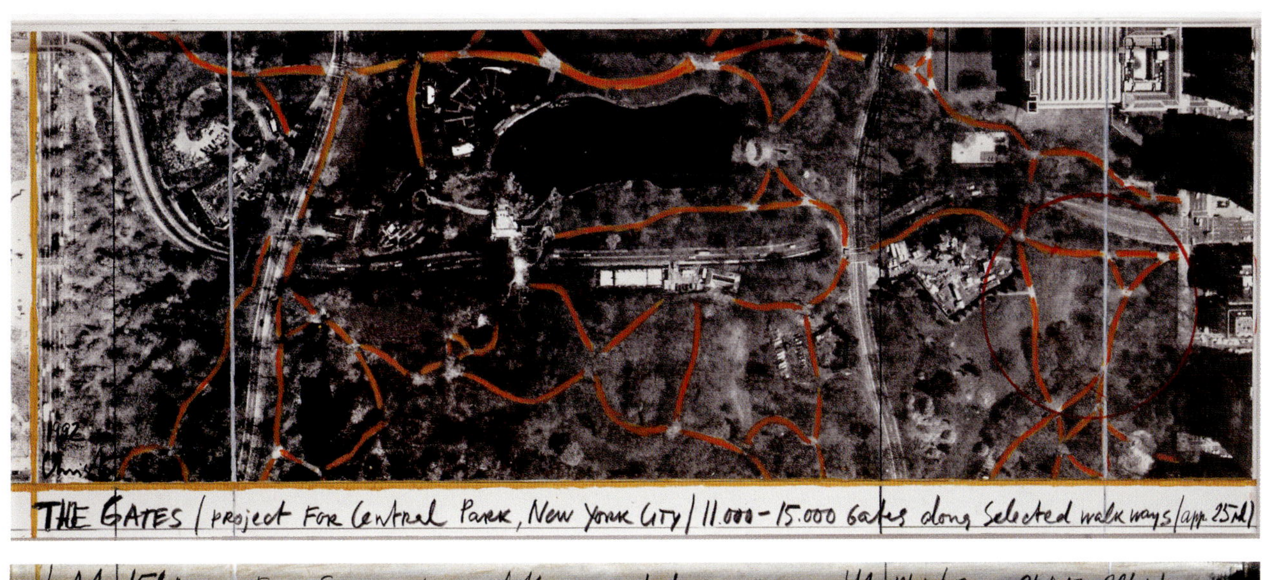
THE GATES / project for Central Park, New York City / 11.000-15.000 Gates along Selected walk ways

users. As though casting a glance back at their *Valley Curtain* and at Running Fence, they propose to suspend fabric panels from the tops of the vinyl gates. Visitors will be able to run and walk under the gates, and dream amid them, as the fabric blows in the wind. Over the past four decades, from the *Wrapped Kunsthalle, Bern, 1968*, to *The Pont Neuf Wrapped, Paris, 1975–1985*, to the *Wrapped Reichstag*, *Berlin, 1971–1995*, the artists have increasingly moved into city spaces. This paid credence to the idea that their work was a kind of temporary landscape art, a new type of garden architecture outside real nature, a pure construct. It can now be seen to have always been profoundly urban, an art that opens up new perspectives to all city dwellers, regardless of age, race, or religion. Like their previous projects, Christo and Jeanne-Claude's Gates, started in 1979, not only involve formal, self-referential, and innovative elements that add up to a coherent artistic whole; they also address a variety of social problems.

It says a great deal for Reinhold Würth that he has chosen to extend his core collection of works by Christo and Jeanne-Claude by acquiring items related to Christo's early years. *The Wrapped Oil Barrels, 1958/59*, now have a place in the collection, as do the doors of the *Red Store Front* (1964). Christo has never been isolated as an artist. He has always been an active thinker, experimenting with new artistic possibilities. His early, static works operated on the basis of the viewer as a passive recipient of a product created by the artist *ex cathedra*, as it were. Gradually, Christo and Jeanne-Claude involved the spectator as an active participant, as they do so marvelously in *The Gates*. This is a work of art to experience, not to look at. It is not static and one-dimensional, but animated. The wind blows through it as though guided by magical forces, inflating and deflating the fabric panels to establish a constantly changing dialogue between the gates. The panels act as blinds, constantly opening up and closing off views of the sky. To walk through *The Gates* is to experience a work in a continual state of flux. Encompassing a shift from stillness to motion, from small objects to extreme monumentality (documented in Wolfgang Volz's wonderful photographs), there is a vast range to Christo and

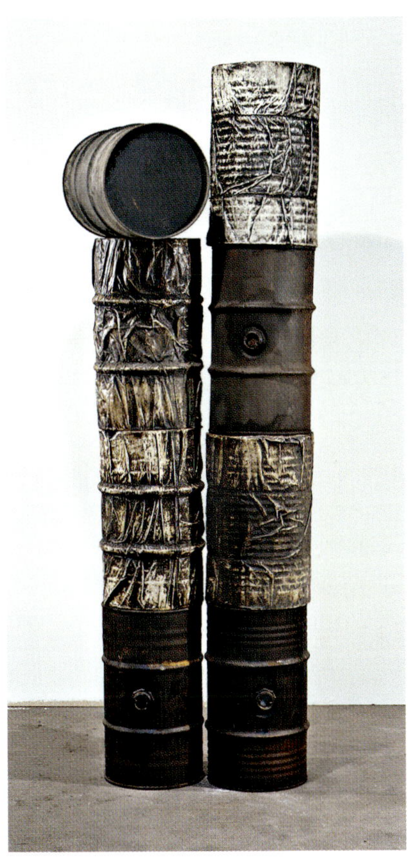

Wrapped Oil Barrels, 1958/59
Lacquered fabric, steel wire, 4 wrapped oil barrels, 4 not wrapped 8 barrels (ca. 39 ½ in. each)
Photo: Wolfgand Voltz

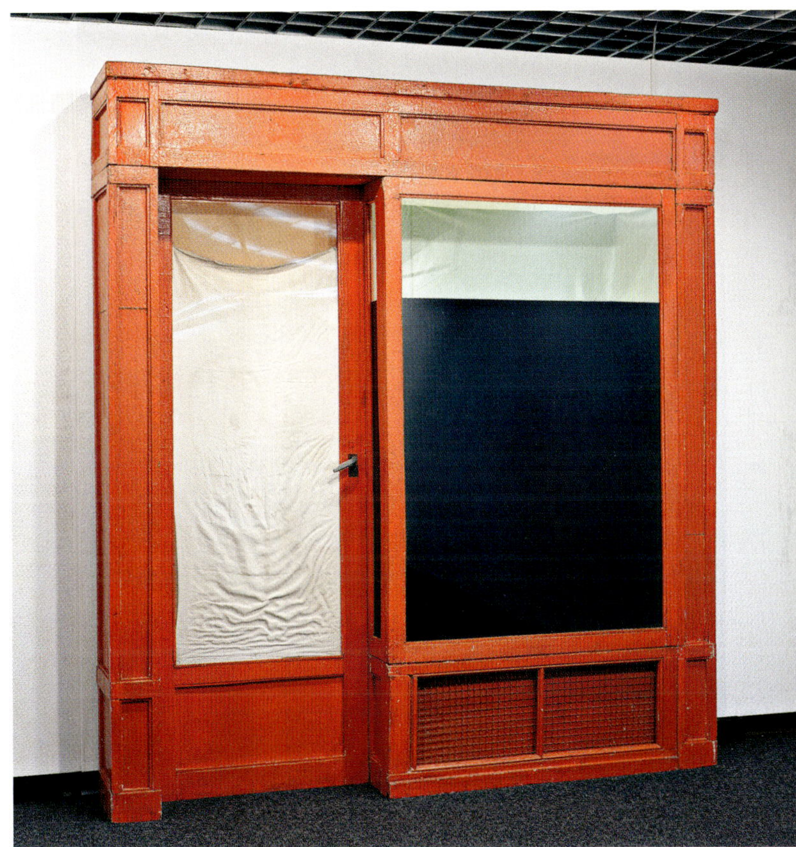

Red Store Front, 1964
Wood, Plexiglas, enamel paint, steel mesh, fabric and electric light, 1964
88 ½ x 82 ⅝ x 13 ¾ in.
Photo: Wolfgand Voltz

Jeanne-Claude's oeuvre. Christo uses photographs, he draws, he makes collages, and he employs industrial materials not automatically associated with 'art'. Christo and Jeanne-Claude devise the concepts they probe their economic, political, and logistical feasibility.

It is hardly surprising that a company executive like Reinhold Würth should be fascinated by the works of two artists that entails exceptional entrepreneurial skills. Both the collector and the artists are guided by a similar vision of creativity and self-fulfillment. They view their activity as meaningful and; they assume that society requires creative, innovative and enterprising individuals to act in an exemplary way by exercising their imagination to break rules, ignore taboos, and adjust tradition in the interests of the future. "Exemplary" here means being different from everybody else, having the courage to make predictions, getting things done whatever the risks involved, and yet doing so in a responsible, considered way, eliminating errors and avoiding disasters.

Reinhold Würth has completely overhauled his company to make it a modern, tertiary sector business. Such a radical departure from previous approaches also characterizes Christo and Jeanne-Claude's move away from traditional visual media to embrace materials generally regarded as industrial – a way of showing that in art other truths pertain. Both the executive/collector and the artists have established a new set of rules for themselves and their activity. Rather than being executors who constantly repeat and imitate themselves, both are well springs of almost volcanic energy who believe in the possibility of altering existing conditions.

"Conditions" for Christo and Jeanne-Claude are not internal factors governing a work of art, like the interaction of color described by Josef Albers. These artists take their points of reference from outside and expand them to create a different kind of aesthetic and artistic experience. That is a basic feature of their entire oeuvre. They are not interested in possible applications of their works; they are engaged in a search for freedom that can achieve the status of truth only in an artistic context. This belief in the freedom of art and in the art of freedom has biographical roots. Christo left Communist Bulgaria for western Europe, before moving to the U.S.A. Jeanne-Claude grew up in France and Switzerland in a household run with the mathematical precision of a military operation. Together, they have established a realm constructed from new perspectives on the world.

This should not be taken to mean that Christo sees his work in completely ahistorical terms. In this context, art historians and classical archaeologists will be reminded of such large-scale architectural ensembles as Gianlorenzo Bernini's colonnade outside St. Peter's in Rome and the grid system of urban planning employed by the Romans, which allowed for expansion by the repetition of basic units. Gardens also come to mind, from classical antiquity to modern times. One thinks especially of French baroque gardens, those grand compositions articulated by landscaped areas. These, too, are governed by repetition, by a kind of fugal construction reminiscent of Bach's music that fashions something big from small units. In 1988 Christo himself noted parallels between his work and the Cubist collages of Picasso and Braque, particularly those of 1913 and 1914: "They sometimes used pieces of newspapers in their collages. The headlines represented something, but these artists appropriated the graphic design of the letters to add an abstract dimension to their work." To paraphrase from the same interview, Christo said: in the same way, one should see that we borrow space which does not belong to art and make it "art space" in our type of sculpture. The essence of our projects is the manipulation of space. The objects or spaces that we use for our projects have already been designed, or are already in a space which has been manipulated by somebody else. Somebody – a politician, an architect, and urban designer, etc. – designed the streets, the highways, the bridges, even the airways. These spaced are utilized by thousands of people who are not aware that someone has designed everything around them. We take all that for granted, even though the space is regulated in a very precise way. We come to that space and suddenly we create a gentle disturbance. By creating new borders, territories, separations, and divisions, we cause people to readjust their movements in that space."[3]

It is impossible to imagine the art world without Christo and Jeanne-Claude. These *sui generis* artists have undertaken a unique journey into new perceptual realms, into what Petra Kipphoff has called the "eternity of the moment."[4] The many published volumes of photographs recording their work testify to the character of each project as an event. These visual documents should not cause us to forget that the artists' organizational activity requires vast amounts of energy and imagination and an extraordinary degree of stamina. It was no doubt this that caused Kipphoff to remark that Christo and Jeanne-Claude are not so much artists as adventurers in the cause of enlightenment. They work *with* things, not *on* them. They stage pieces of pure poetry, they expand experience. Christo wraps objects such as *Wrapped Violin, 1994*. Every project is choreographed as a single entity.

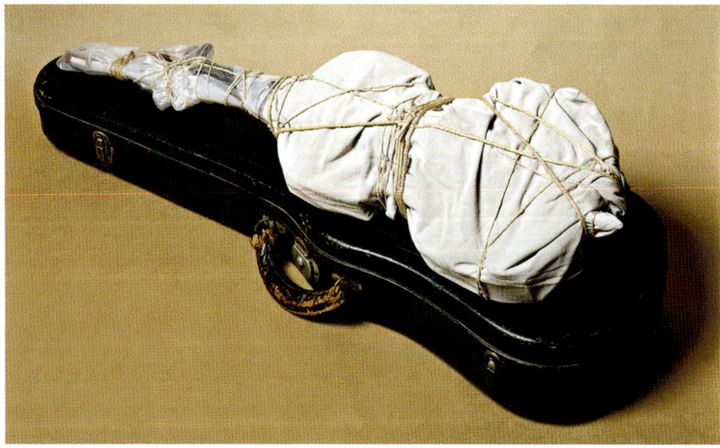

Wrapped Violin
Violin, fabric, plastic (with black crate of violin), 1994
3 ⅞ x 29 ½ x 9 ⅛ in. (violin)
4 ⅞ x 30 ¼ x 11 in. (crate)

The concept underlying the artists' work might be described as "uncovering by covering." *The Gates* will involve the entire Central Park. They echo and redefine the contours of the walkways of the park. They harmonize with the shapes of the trees and other vegetation. They are a series of individual interventions, placed at the mercy of the weather. This differs from the irony evident in the *Oil Barrels* and from the critique of the packaging industry and its aesthetics that informed *Black Box*, works that tended to direct attention away from the wrapped object. Christo and Jeanne-Claude have now turned to addressing other optical experiences, sets of interrelations that generate associative thought processes in the course of walking in and through a work of art. These artists have changed the world of art by bursting the existing bounds of artistic practice. At a time when Color Field painting, Minimalism, shaped canvases, and non-relational forms dominated art, a young man arrived from Bulgaria and, along with his contemporaries, the Nouveaux Réalistes – Arman, César, Yves Klein, Niki de St. Phalle, Daniel Spoerri, Jean Tinguely – proceeded to do away with an art that was no longer interested in representation. This entry into new artistic territory occurred at the same time as Pop Art in the United States, which likewise ignored all desires for abstraction and the pressures to practice it in order to embrace a new approach to representation.

Ultimately, the explosive effect of Christo and Jeanne-Claude's work has been greater than that of all these artists. They have remained true to themselves, constructing a legacy that will live on in the form of studies and documentation. The early objects still exist, as do marvelous documentary photographs of projects and sketches of them before and after their realization. Christo and Jeanne-Claude have worked on a previously inconceivable scale. They are not powerful figures of the kind who could command the construction of the Great Wall of China; they are artists who would diligently and conscientiously give it new significance. The work of Christo and Jeanne-Claude is transparent in meaning and does not advance a single view. It is therefore actively democratic.

Dieter Ronte, Bonn, August 2004

Notes

1 Bertolt Brecht, *Schriften zur Literatur und Kunst*, vol. 2: 1920–1939 (Berlin and Weimar, 1966), quoted in *Realismus*, exh. cat., Hamburg, 1978–1979.

2 D. Burdon, O. Hahn, and P. Restany, *Christo* (Milan: Edition Apollinaire, 1965)

3 Quoted in Masahiko Yanagi, "Interview with Christo", in *Christo: The Umbrellas, Joint Project for Japan and USA, Drawings and Collages* (London, Annely Juda Fine Art, London 1988)

4 Petra Kipphoff, *Christo, Künstler*, Kritisches Lexikon der Gegenwartskunst, vol. 20 (Munich: Weltkunst und Bruckmann, 1992).

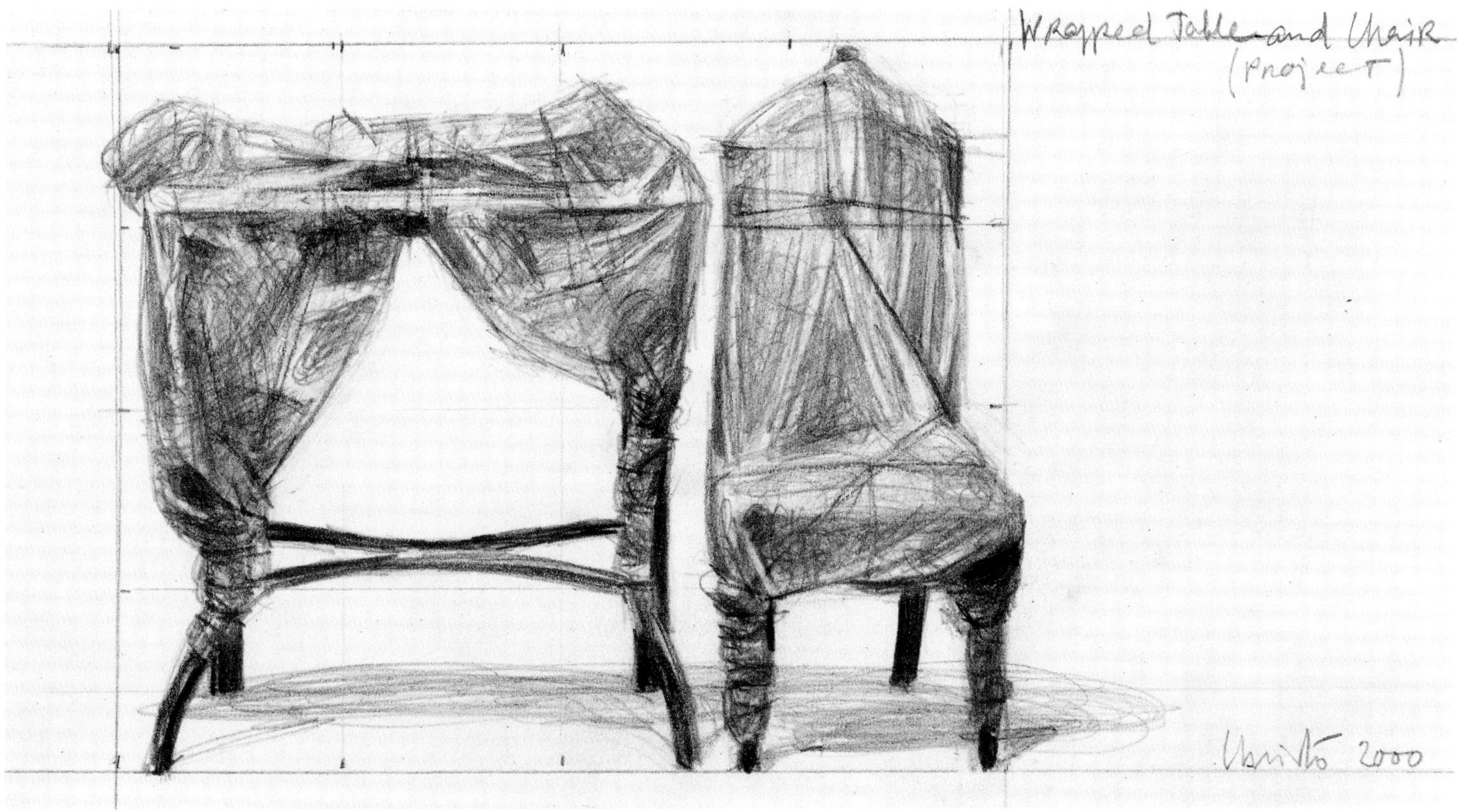

Wrapped Table and Chair (Project)
Crayon and pastel on cardboard
8 ⅞ x 4 ¾ in.

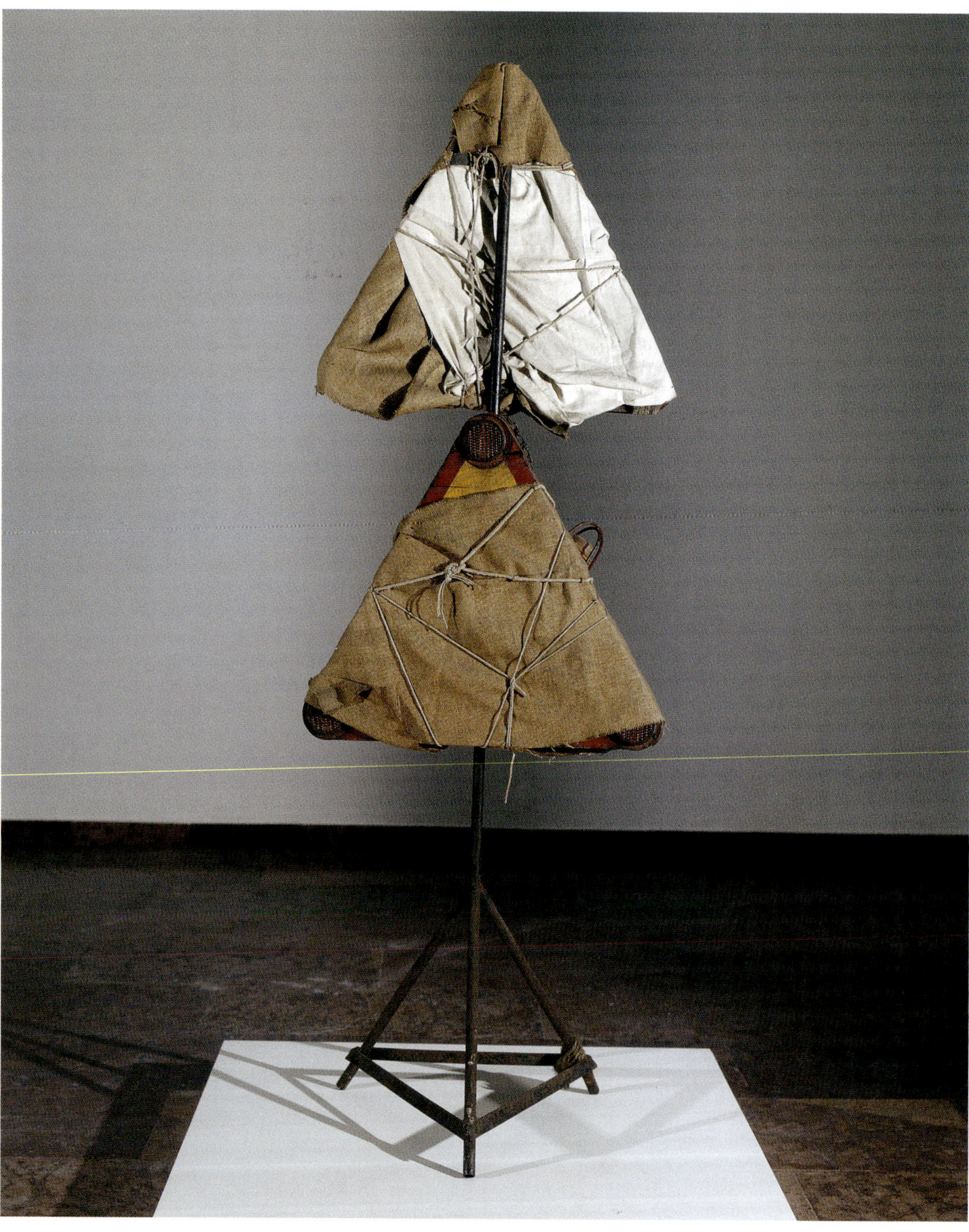

Wrapped Road Sign, 1963
Wooden traffic sign, signal lamp, fabric, jute, and rope on metal stand
71 ¼ x 24 ⅝ x 18 ½ in.

CATALOGUE ENTRIES

EARLY WORKS

Between 1964 and 1967 Christo created a series of architectural scale sculptures in the shape of store fronts.

They were an extension of the 1962 *Show Cases* and the 1963 *Show Windows*. Unlike his previous works he used both the inner space and the outer space.

In commercial store fronts the exterior facade is made for interior display. In Christo's "Store Fronts", the life-size glass windows are partially covered, on the inside surface of the glass, with either fabric, paint or wrapping paper, thereby preventing the standing or walking viewerfrom seeing the inside spaceand left to wonder about the content of the inside space which is illuminated and slightly visible.

The use of inner/outer space became evident in Christo and Jeanne-Claude's temporary environmental works of art such as: *The Umbrellas*, Japan-USA 1984–1991 and the two works in progress: *The Gates, Project for Central Park, New York City*, which was started in 1979, and in *Over The River, Project for the Arkansas River, Colorado*, which was started in 1992.

Before actually building a life-size "Store Front", Christo always made preparatory sketches, collages, drawings and scale models.

The last one in the Store Fronts series was the *Corridor Store Front, 1967,* which covered a surface of 1,500 square feet.

"The showcases mark a decisive shift in Christo's development. They led to the store fronts and architectural scale, freeing him from dependency on pre-existent objects and enabling him to package invented shapes and empty spaces of any size he wanted.... Like facades on a movie set, the store-front sculptures have real architectural scale without being real buildings. The perversity of having an architectural exterior displayed indoors is compounded by the enigmatically draped windows... Although doors can admit symbolic interpretation, Christo's locked entrances remind us that we are shut out on our side of his store fronts.... Yet the veiled windows attract the most attention. Throughout the ages, windows have held a special fascination for painters, because they provide spatial and temporal cross-references between indoor and outdoor settings and activities. In addition to contributing formal complexity, windows have a psychological quality that invites symbolic use...."

From Christo by David Bourdon
Harry N. Abrams Publications, New York, 1970

Show Window, 1965/66
Galvanized metal, aluminum, Plexiglas, brown wrapping paper, Masonite, wood, and tape
84 ⅛ x 48 x 3 ½ in.

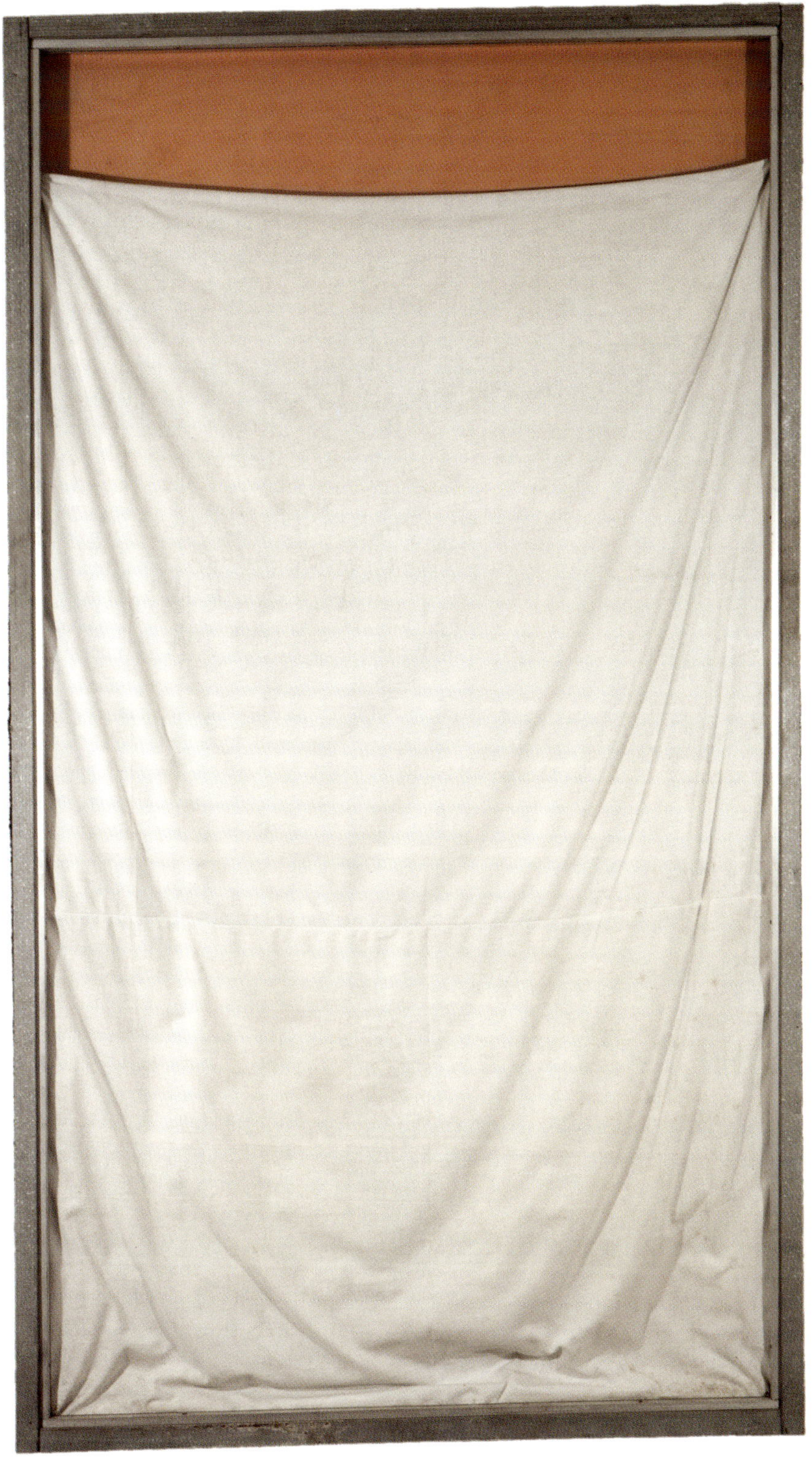

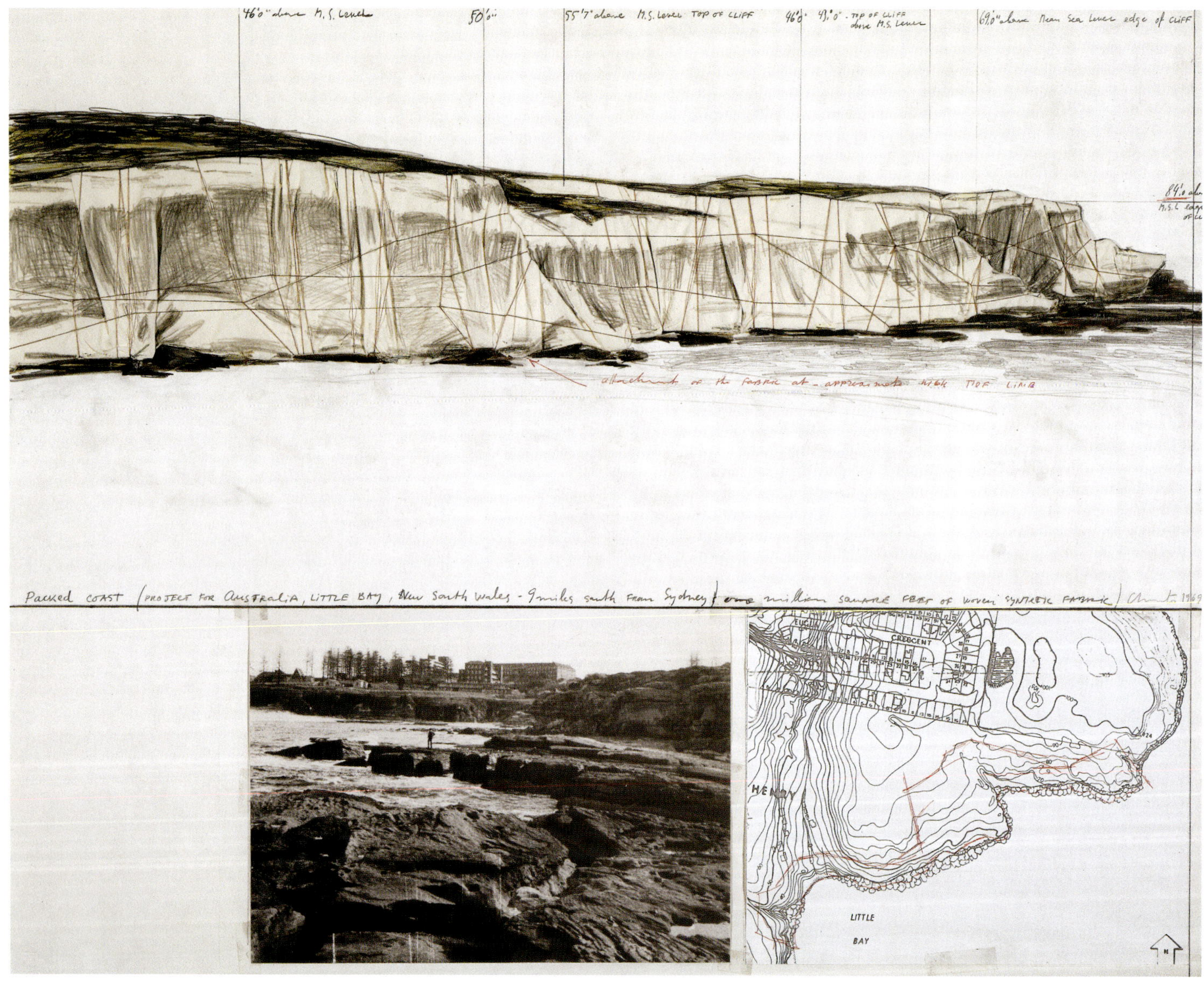

Wrapped Coast, Project for Australia, Little Bay
Collage, 1969
22 x 28 in.

WRAPPED COAST, One Million Square Feet, Little Bay, Australia, 1968–1969

Little Bay, property of Prince Henry Hospital, is located 9 miles (14.5 km), southeast of the center of Sydney.

The cliff-lined shore area that was wrapped is approximately 1.5 miles (2.4 km) long, 150 to 800 ft wide, 85 ft high at the northern cliffs, and was at sea level at the southern sandy beach.

One million square feet of erosion control fabric (synthetic woven fiber usually manufactured for agricultural purposes) was used for the wrapping. 35 miles (56.3 km) of polypropylene rope, ½ in. diameter tied the fabric to the rocks.

Ramset guns fired 25,000 charges of fasteners, threaded studs and clips to secure the rope to the rocks.

Mr. Ninian Melville, a retired major in the Army Corps of Engineers, was in charge of the workers at the site. 17,000 manpower hours, over a period of four weeks, were expended by 15 professional mountain climbers, 110 laborers, architecture and art students from the University of Sydney and East Sydney Technical College, as well as a number of Australian artists and teachers.

The project was financed by Christo and Jeanne-Claude through the sale of Christo's original preparatory drawings and collages.

The coast remained wrapped for a period of seven weeks from October 28, 1969. Then all materials were removed and the site returned to its original condition.

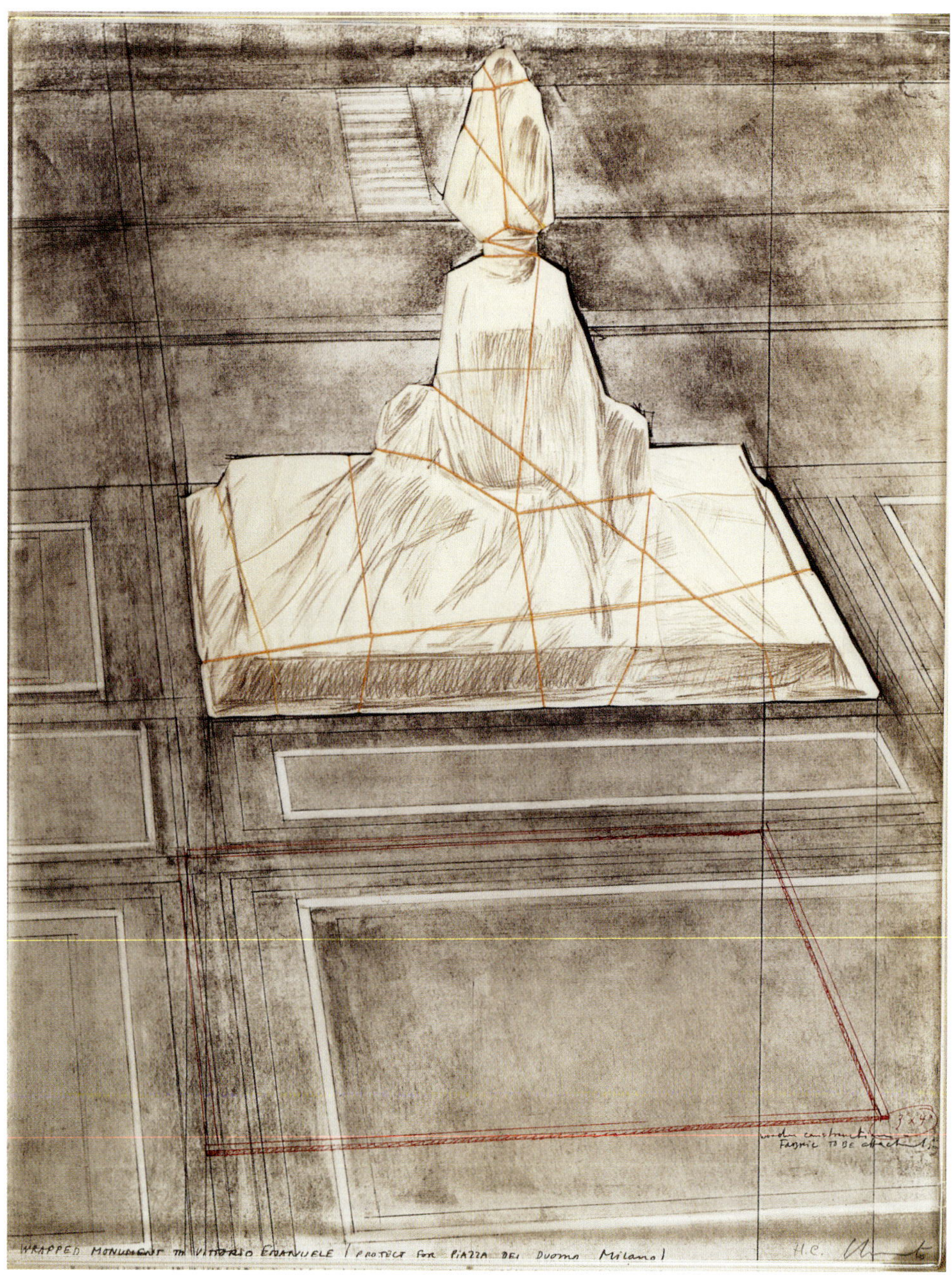

Wrapped Monument to Vittorio Emanuele, Project for Piazza del Duomo, Milano.
Hand-collaged lithograph, 1970–1975
28 x 22 in.

WRAPPED MONUMENTS, Monument to V. Emanuele

The monument to the King of Italy, Vittorio Emanuele, on Piazza del Duomo, and the monument to Leonardo da Vinci, on Piazza della Scala, were wrapped with polypropylene fabric and red polypropylene rope, in the fall of 1970, in Milano, Italy.

The fabric had been sewn beforehand according to patterns, allowing ample folds.

The two wrapped monuments could be seen from the center of the Galleria, simultaneously, at each extremity of the nineteenth-century grand vaulted pedestrian shopping passageway.

The monument to Vittorio Emanuele projected in front of the late nineteenth-century cathedral, the Duomo, while the monument to Leonardo da Vinci was situated in front of the eighteenth-century La Scala theater and the Milano City Hall.

All expenses were born by the artists.

The artists do not accept sponsorship of any kind.

The *Wrapped Monument* to Vittorio Emanuele remained for two days, while the *Wrapped Monument* to Leonardo da Vinci remained for one week.

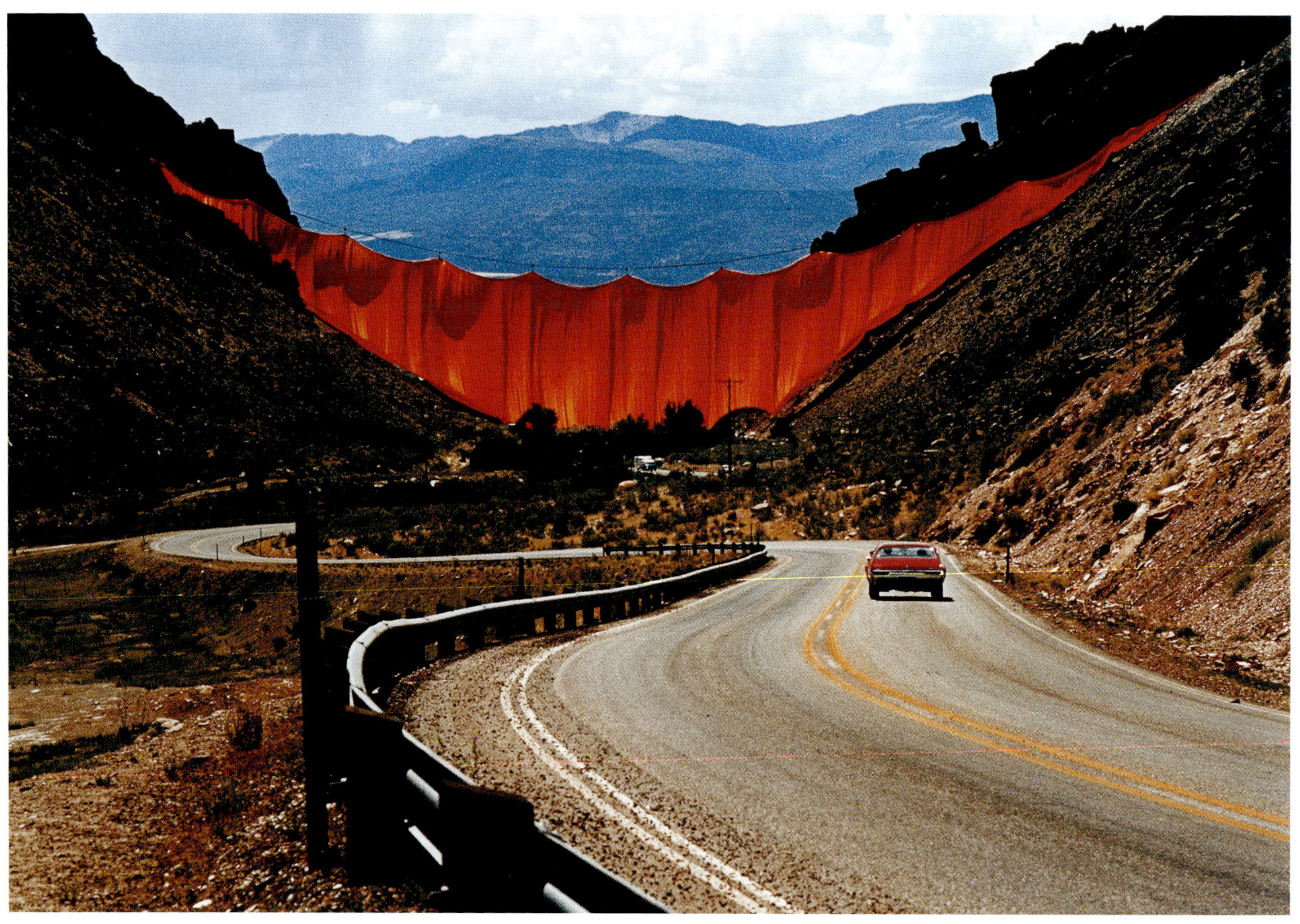

Valley Curtain, Rifle, Colorado, 1970–1972
Photograph
28 x 39 ¾ in.
Photo: Wolfgang Volz

VALLEY CURTAIN, Rifle, Colorado, 1970–1972

On August 10, 1972, in Rifle, Colorado, between Grand Junction and Glenwood Spring in the Grand Hogback Mountain Range, at 11 am, a group of 35 construction workers and 64 temporary helpers, art schools, college students, and itinerant art workers tied down the last of 27 ropes that secured the 142,000 sq ft of woven nylon fabric orange curtain to its moorings at Rifle Gap, seven miles (11.3 km) north of Rifle, on Highway 325.

Valley Curtain was designed by Dimiter Zagoroff and John Thomson of Unipolycon of Lynn, Massachusetts, and Dr. Ernest C. Harris of Ken R. White Company, Denver, Colorado. It was built by A-&-H Builders Inc. of Boulder, Colorado,President, Theodore Dougherty, under the site supervision of Henry B. Leininger.

By suspending the *Valley Curtain*, at a width of 1,250 ft and a height curving from 365 ft at each end to 182 ft at the center, the curtain remained clear of the slopes and the Valley bottom. A 10 ft skirt attached to the lower part of the curtain visually completed the area between the thimbles and the ground.

An outer cocoon enclosed the fully fitted *Valley Curtain* for protection during transit and at the time of its raising into position and securing to the 11 cable clamps connections at the four main upper cables. The cables spanned 1,368 ft, weighed 110,000 lb, and were anchored to792 short tons of concrete foundations.

An inner cocoon, integral to the *Valley Curtain*, provided added insurance. The bottom of the Curtain was laced to a 3 in. diameter dacron rope from which the control and tie-down lines ran to the 27 anchors.

The *Valley Curtain* project took 28 months to complete.

Christo and Jeanne-Claude's temporary work of art was financed by the Valley Curtain Corporation (Jeanne-Claude Christo-Javacheff, President) through the sale of the studies, preparatory drawings and collages, scale models, early works, and original lithographs.

On August 11, 1972, 28 hours after completion of the project, a gale estimated in excess of 100 kph (60 mph) made it necessary to start the removal.

Valley Curtain, Project for Rifle, Colorado
Collage, 1972
28 x 22 in.

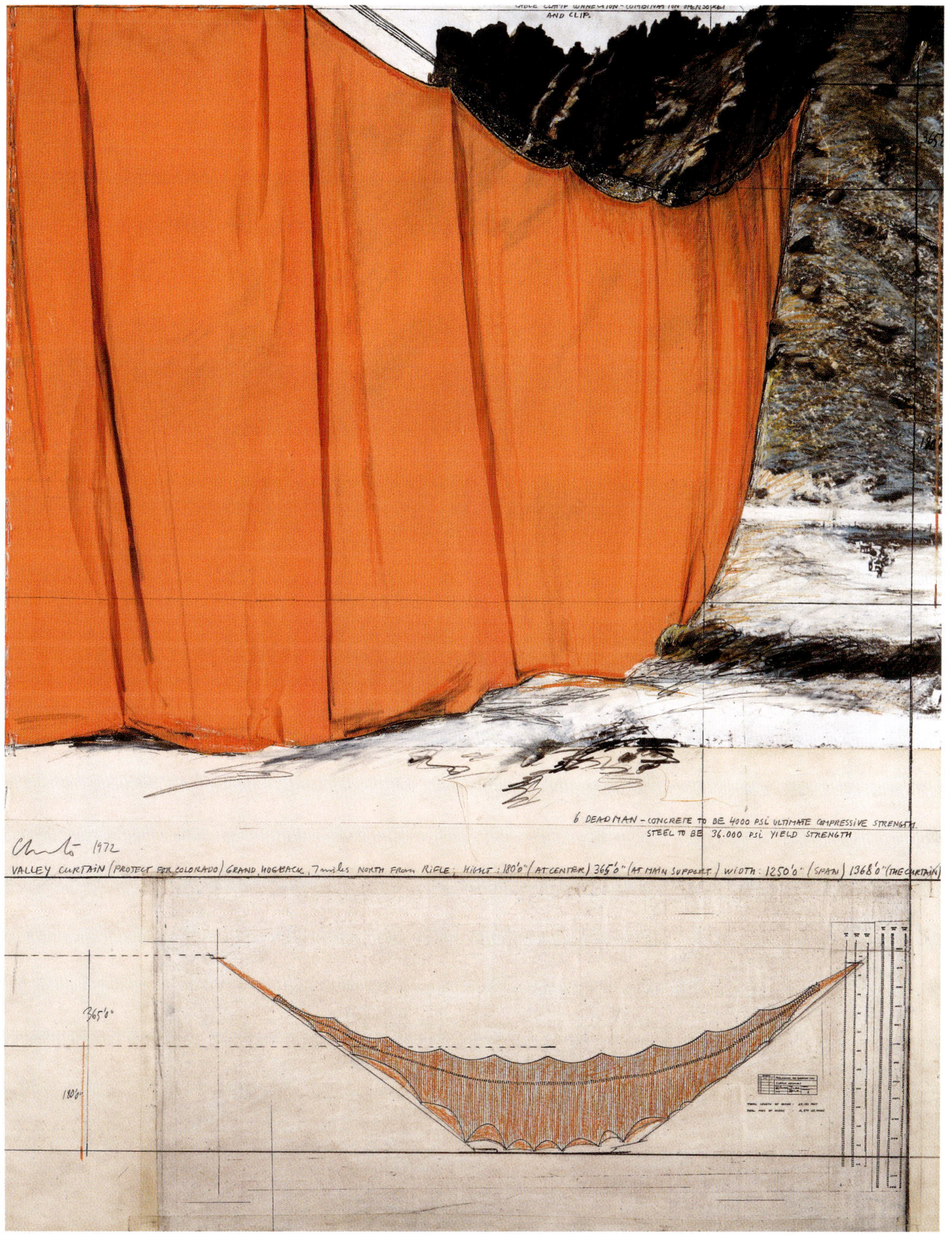
AND CLIP.
6 DEADMAN - CONCRETE TO BE 4000 PSI ULTIMATE COMPRESSIVE STRENGTH.
STEEL TO BE 36.000 PSI YIELD STRENGTH
1972
VALLEY CURTAIN (PROJECT FOR COLORADO) GRAND HOGBACK, 7 miles NORTH FROM RIFLE; HIGHT: 180'0" (AT CENTER) 365'0" (AT MAIN SUPPORT) WIDTH: 1250'0" (SPAN) 1368'0" (THE CURTAIN)
365'0"
180'0"

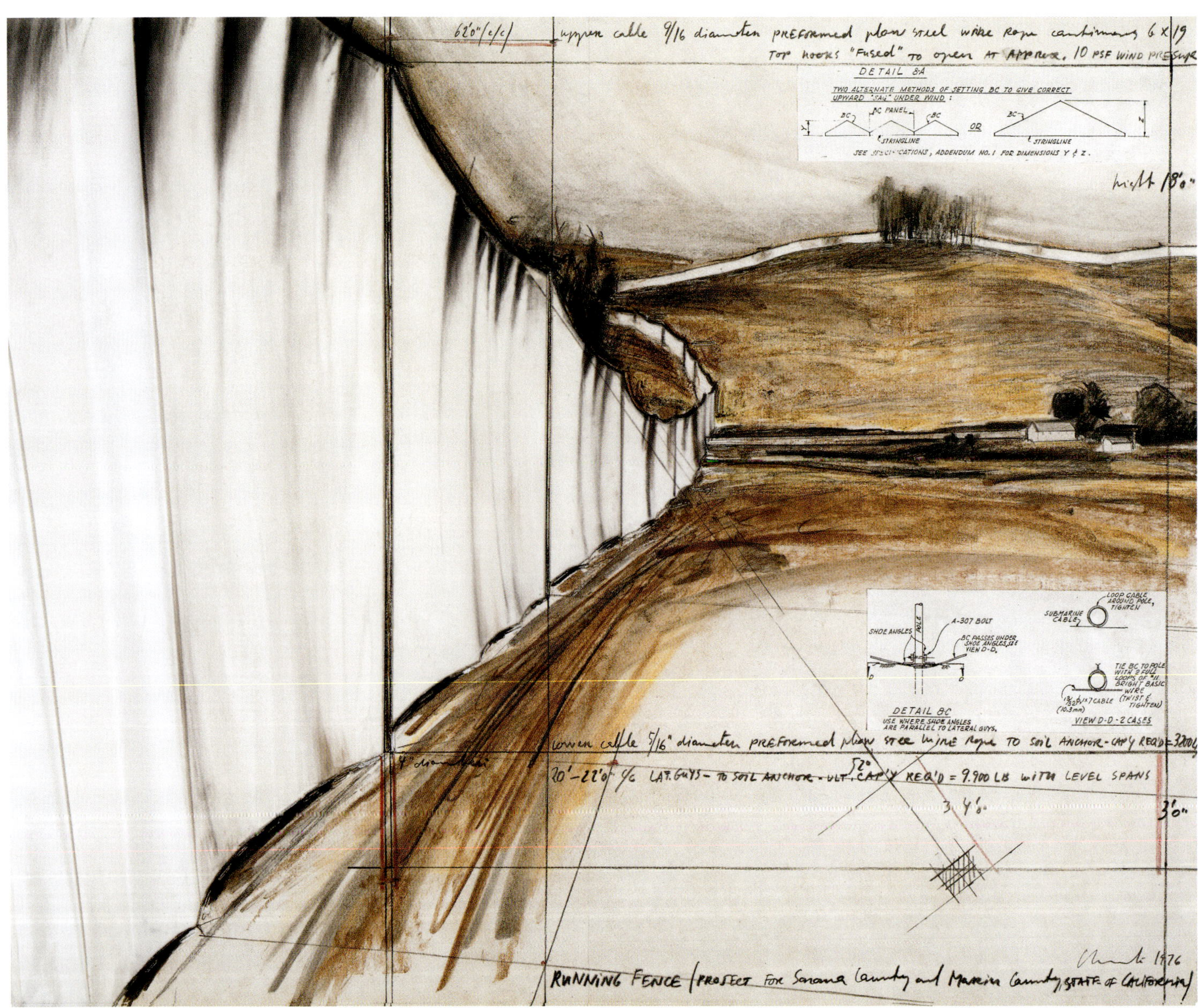

Running Fence, Project for Sonoma and Marin Counties, California
Collage, 1976
22 x 28 in.

RUNNING FENCE, Sonoma and Marin Counties, California 1972–1976

Running Fence, 18 ft high, 24 ½ miles (40 km) long, extending East-West near Freeway 101, north of San Francisco, on the private properties of 59 ranchers, following rolling hills and dropping down to the Pacific Ocean at Bodega Bay, was completed on September 10, 1976.

The art project consisted of 42 months of collaborative efforts, the ranchers' participation, 18 public hearings, three sessions at the Superior Courts of California, the drafting of a 450-page Environmental Impact Report and the temporary use of hills, the sky and the Ocean.

All expenses for the temporary work of art were paid by Christo and Jeanne-Claude through the sale of studies, preparatory drawings and collages, scale models and original lithographs.

Running Fence was made of 2,222,222 sq ft of heavy woven white nylon fabric, hung from a steel cable strung between 2,050 steel poles (each 21 ft long, diameter 3 ½ in.) embedded 3 ft into the ground, using no concrete and braced laterally with guy wires, 90 miles (145 km) of steel cable and 14,000 earth anchors.

The top and bottom edges of the 2,050 fabric panels were secured to the upper and lower cables by 350,000 hooks.

All parts of *Running Fence*'s structure were designed for complete removal and no visible evidence of *Running Fence* remains on the hills of Sonoma and Marin Counties.

As it had been agreed with the ranchers and with the County, State and Federal Agencies, the removal of *Running Fence* started 14 days after its completion and all materials were given to the ranchers.

Running Fence crossed 14 roads and the town of Valley Ford, leaving passage for cars, cattle and wildlife, and was designed to be viewed by following 65 km (40 miles) of public roads, in Sonoma and Marin Counties.

Running Fence, Sonoma and Marin Counties, California, 1972–1976
Photograph, 1976
28 x 39 ¾ in.
Photo: Wolfgang Volz

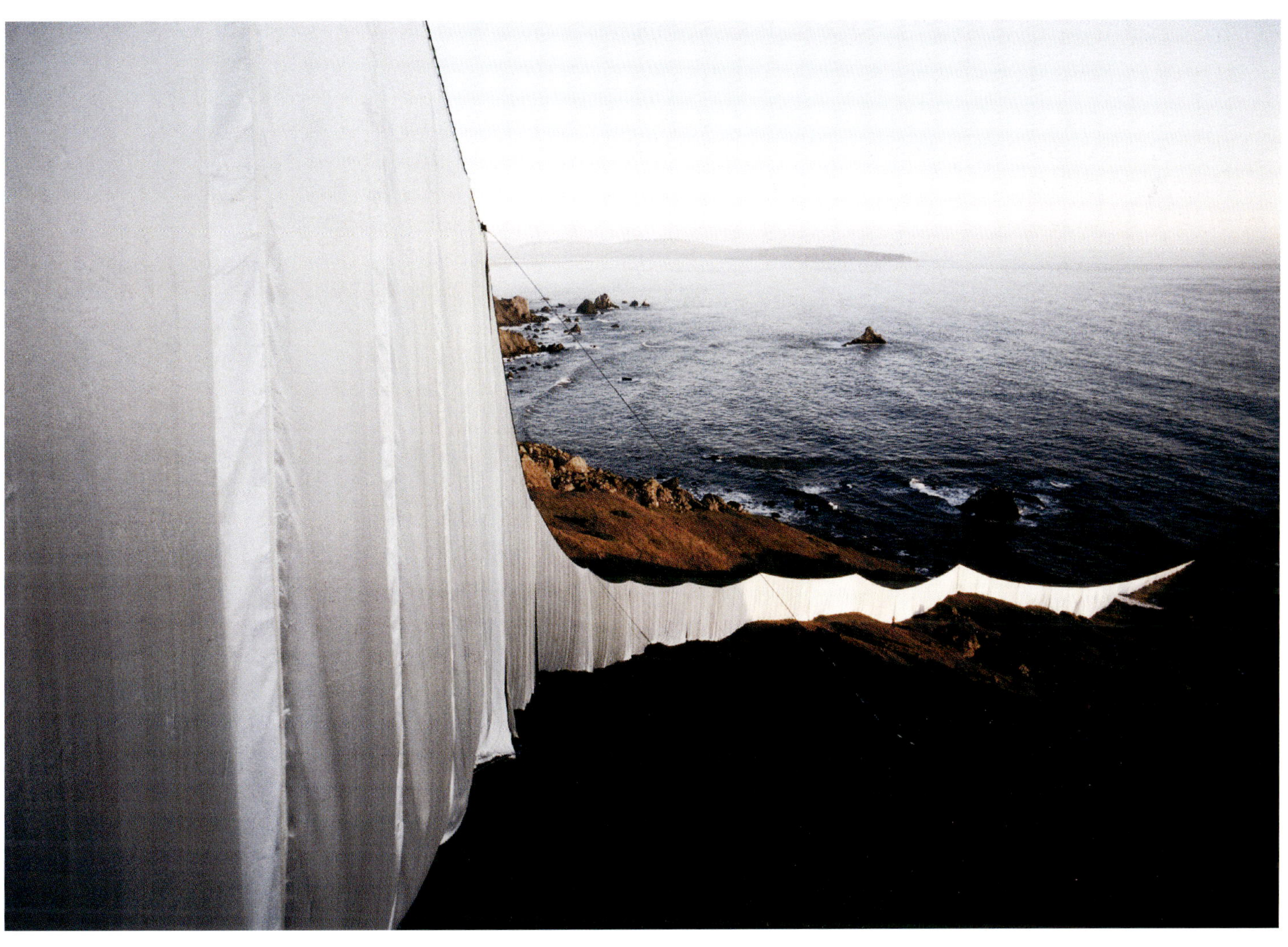

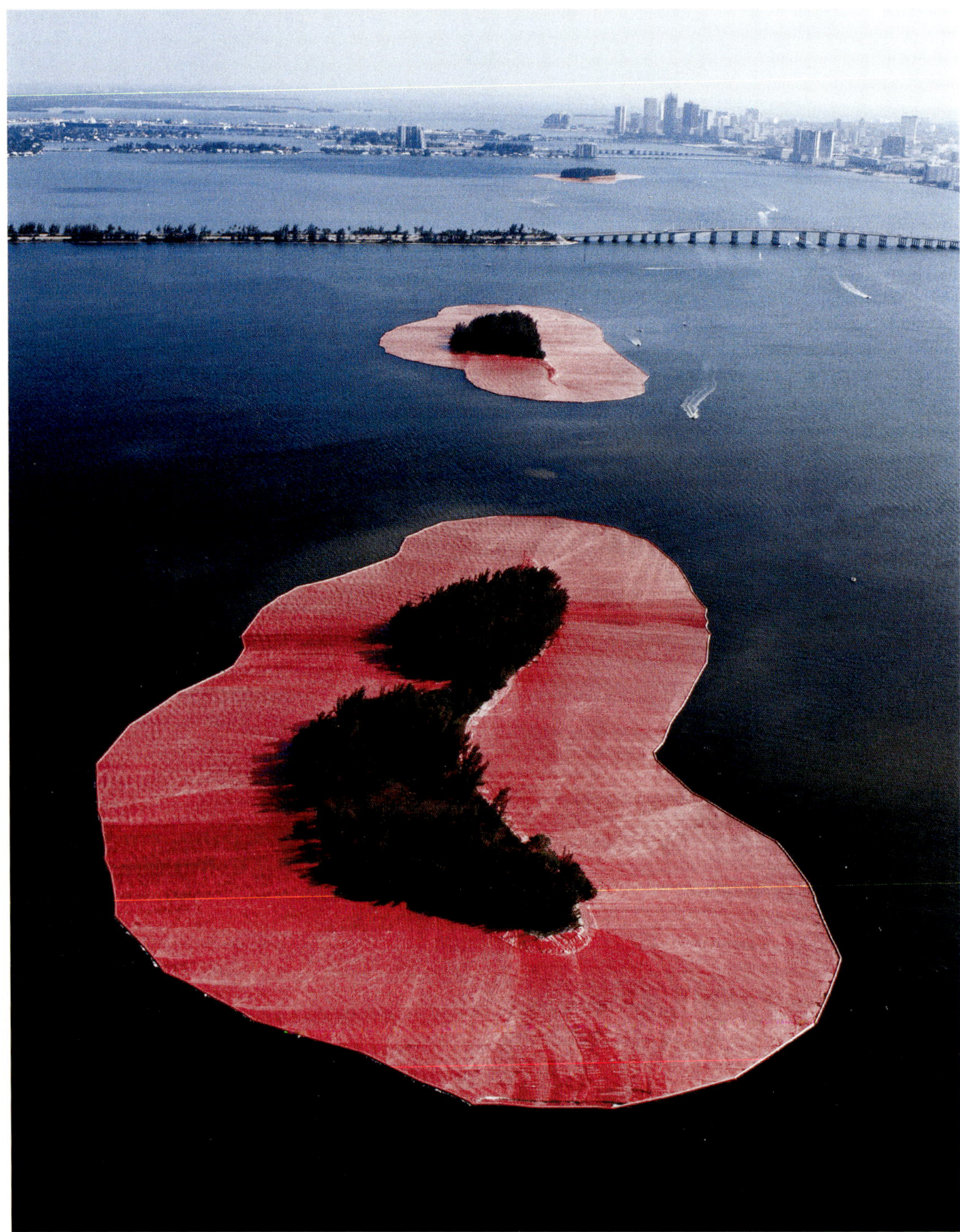

Surrounded Islands, Biscayne Bay, Greater Miami, Florida 1980–1983
Photograph, 1983
39 ¾ x 28 in.
Photo: Wolfgang Volz

SURROUNDED ISLANDS, Biscayne Bay, Miami, Florida, 1980–1983

On May 7, 1983 the installation of *Surrounded Islands* was completed. In Biscayne Bay, between the city of Miami, North Miami, the Village of Miami Shores and Miami Beach, 11 of the islands situated in the area of Bakers Haulover Cut, Broad Causeway, 79th Street Causeway, Julia Tuttle Causeway, and Venetian Causeway were surrounded with 6.5 million sq ft of pink woven polypropylene fabric covering the surface of the water, floating and extending out 200 ft from each island into the Bay. The fabric was sewn into 79 patterns to follow the contours of the 11 islands.

For two weeks *Surrounded Islands,* spreading over 7 miles (11.3 km) was seen, approached and enjoyed by the public, from the causeways, the land, the water and the air. The luminous pink color of the shiny fabric was in harmony with the tropical vegetation of the uninhabited verdant island, the light of the Miami sky and the colors of the shallow waters of Biscayne Bay.

Since April 1981, attorneys Joseph Z. Fleming, Joseph W. Landers, marine biologist Dr. Anitra Thorhaug, ornithologists Dr. Oscar Owre and Meri Cummings, mammal expert Dr. Daniel Odell, marine engineer John Michel, four consulting engineers, and builder-contractor, Ted Dougherty of A & H Builders,Inc. had been working on the preparation of the *Surrounded Islands*. The marine and land crews picked up debris from the eleven islands, putting refuse in bags and carting it away after they had removed some 40 tons of varied garbage: refrigerator doors, tires, kitchen sinks, mattresses and an abandoned boat.

Permits were obtained from the following governmental agencies: The Governor of Florida and the Cabinet; and the Dade County Commission; the Department of Environmental Regulation; the City of Miami Commission; the City of North Miami; the Village of Miami Shores; the U.S. Army Corps of Engineers; the Dade County Department of Environmental Resources Management.

From November 1982 until April 1983, 6,500,000 square feet of woven polypropylene fabric were sewn at the rented Hialeah factory, into 79 different patterns to follow the contours of the 11 islands. A flotation strip was sewn in each seam. At the Opa Locka Blimp Hangar, the sewn sections were accordion folded to ease the unfurling on the water.

The outer edge of the floating fabric was attached to a 12 in. diameter octagonal boom, in sections, of the same color as the fabric. The boom was connected to the radial anchor lines which extended from the anchors at the island to the 610 specially made anchors, spaced at 50 ft intervals, 250 ft beyond the perimeter of each island, driven into the limestone at the bottom of the Bay. Earth anchors were driven into the land, near the foot of the trees, to secure the inland edge of the fabric, covering the surface of the beach and disappearing under the vegetation.

The floating rafts of fabric and booms, varying from 12 to 22 ft in width and from 400 to 600 ft in length were towed through the Bay to each island. There were 11 islands, but on two occasions, two islands were surrounded together as one configuration.

As with Christo and Jeanne-Claude's previous art projects, Surrounded Islands was entirely financed by the artists, through the sale by C.V.J. Corporation (Jeanne-Claude Christo-Javacheff, President) of the preparatory pastel and charcoal drawings, collages, lithographs and early works.

On May 4, 1983, out of a total work force of 430, the unfurling crew began to blossom the pink fabric. *Surrounded Islands* was tended day and night by 120 monitors in inflatable boats.

Surrounded Islands was a work of art which underlined the various elements and ways in which the people of Miami live, between land and water.

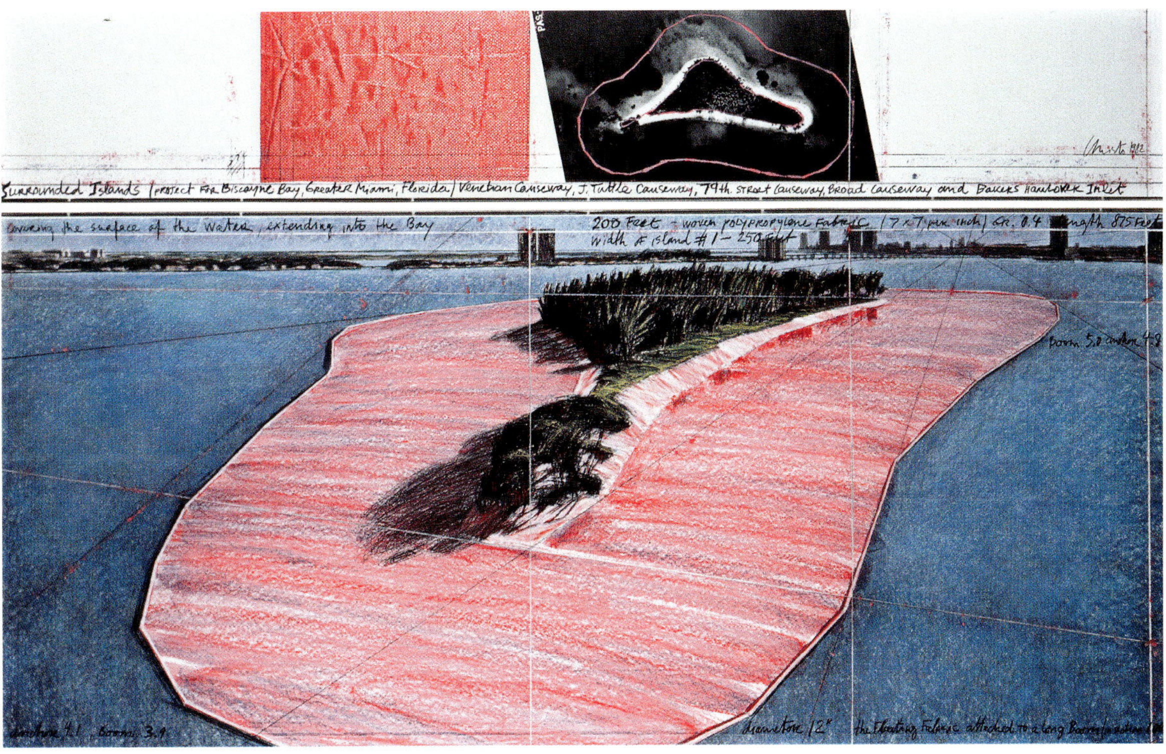

Surrounded Islands, Project for Biscayne Bay, Greater Miami, Florida
Drawing (in two parts), 1982
15 x 96 in., 42 x 96 in.

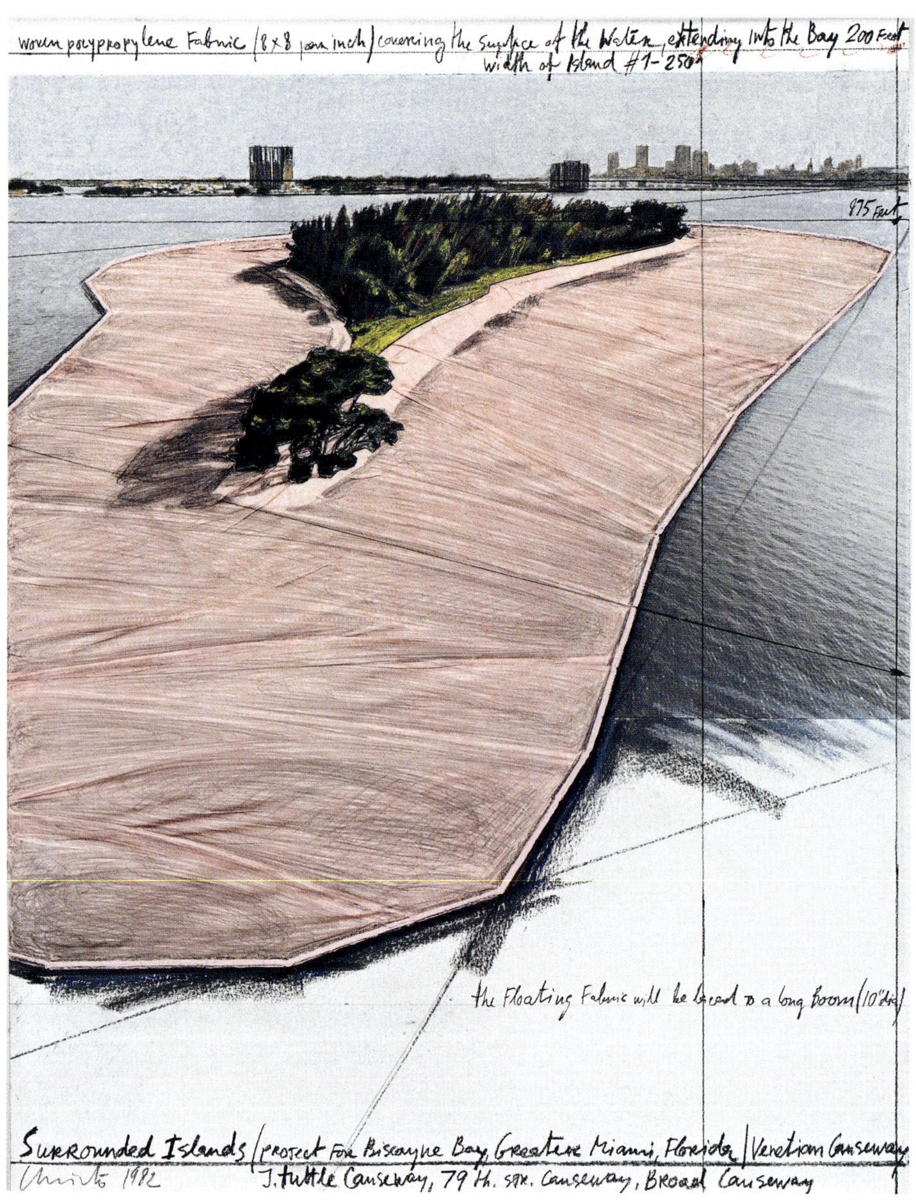

Surrounded Islands, Project for Biscayne Bay, Greater Miami, Florida
Collage, 1982
28 x 22 in.

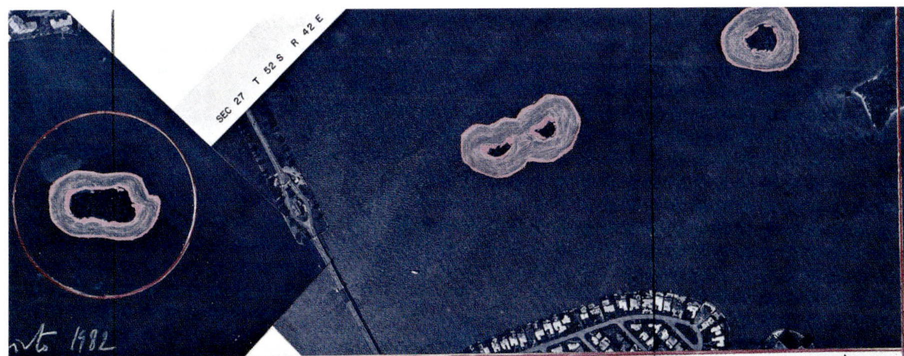

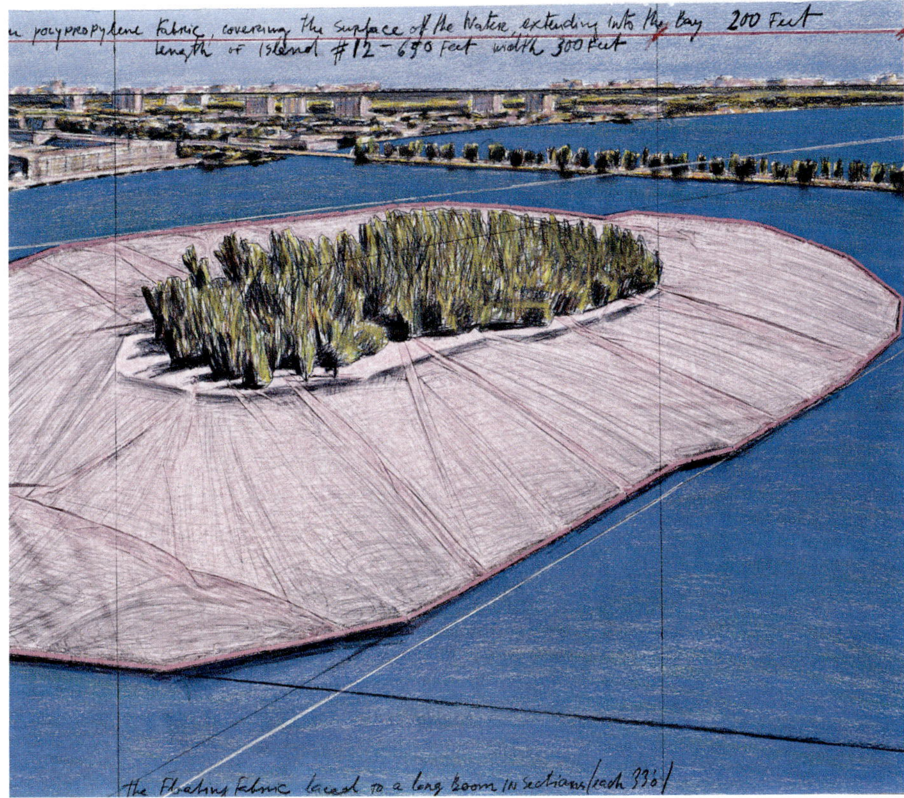

Surrounded Islands, Project for Biscayne Bay, Greater Miami, Florida
Collage (in two parts), 1982
11 x 28 in., 22 x 28 in.

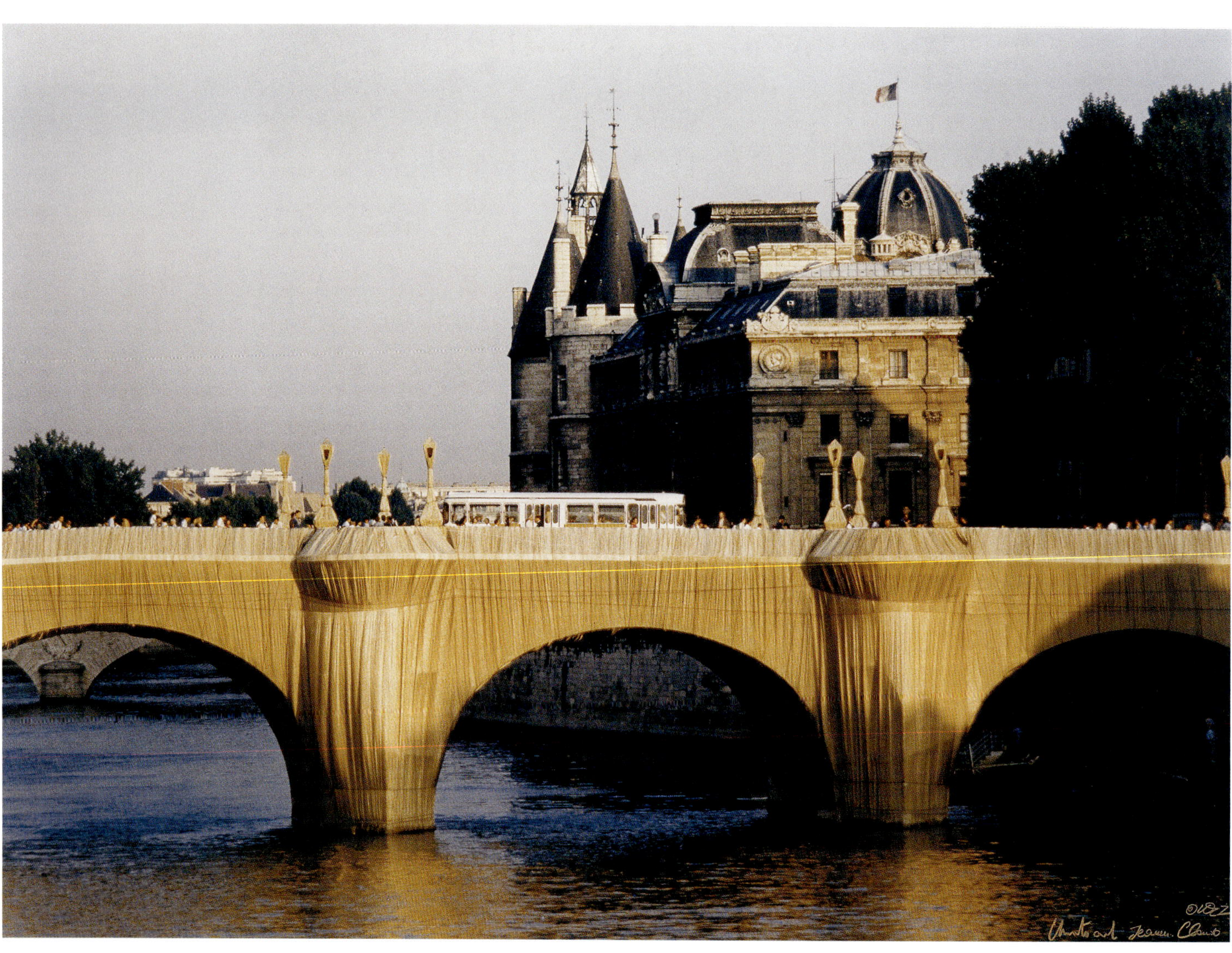

THE PONT NEUF WRAPPED, Paris, 1975–1985

On September 22, 1985, a group of 300 professional workers completed the temporary work of art *The Pont Neuf Wrapped.* They had deployed 454,178 sq ft of woven polyamide fabric, silky in appearance and golden sandstone in color, covering:

- The sides and vaults of the twelve arches, without hindering river traffic.
- The parapets down to the ground.
- The sidewalks and curbs (pedestrians walked on the fabric).
- All the street lamps on both sides of the bridge.
- The vertical part of the embankment of the western tip of the Ile de la Cité.
- The esplanade of the "Vert-Galant".

The fabric was restrained by 42,900 ft of rope and secured by 11.8 long tons of steel chains encircling the base of each tower, 3.3 ft underwater.

The "Charpentiers de Paris" headed by Gérard Moulin, with French sub-contractors, were assisted by the USA engineers who have worked on Christo and Jeanne-Claude's previous projects, under the direction of Theodore Dougherty: Vahé Aprahamian, August L. Huber, James Fuller, John Thomson and Dimiter Zagoroff.

The Pont Neuf Wrapped, Paris, 1975–1985
Photograph, 1985
28 x 39 ¾ in.
Photo: Wolfgang Volz

Johannes Schaub, the project's director, had submitted the work method and detailed plans and received approval for the project from the authorities of the City of Paris, the Departement of the Seine and the State.

600 monitors, in crews of 40, lead by Simon Chaput, were working around the clock maintaining the project and giving information, until the removal of the project on October 7.

All expenses for *The Pont Neuf Wrapped* were borne by the artists as in their other projects through the sale of preparatory drawings and collages as well as earlier works.

Begun under Henry III, the Pont-Neuf was completed in July 1606, during the reign of Henry IV. No other bridge in Paris offers such topographical and visual variety, today as in the past. From 1578 to 1890, the Pont Neuf underwent continual changes and additions of the most extravagant sort, such as the construction of shops on the bridge under Soufflot, the building, demolition, rebuilding and once again demolition of the massive rococco structure which housed the Samaritaine's water pump. Wrapping the Pont-Neuf continues this tradition of successive metamorphoses by a new sculptural dimension and transforms it, for 14 days, into a work of art.

Ropes held down the fabric to the bridge's surface and maintained the principal shapes, accentuating relief while emphasizing proportions and details of the Pont-Neuf which joins the left and right banks and the Ile de la Cité, the heart of Paris for over two thousand years.

The Pont Neuf Wrapped, Project for Paris
Collage (in two parts), 1980
11 x 28 in., 22 x 28 in.

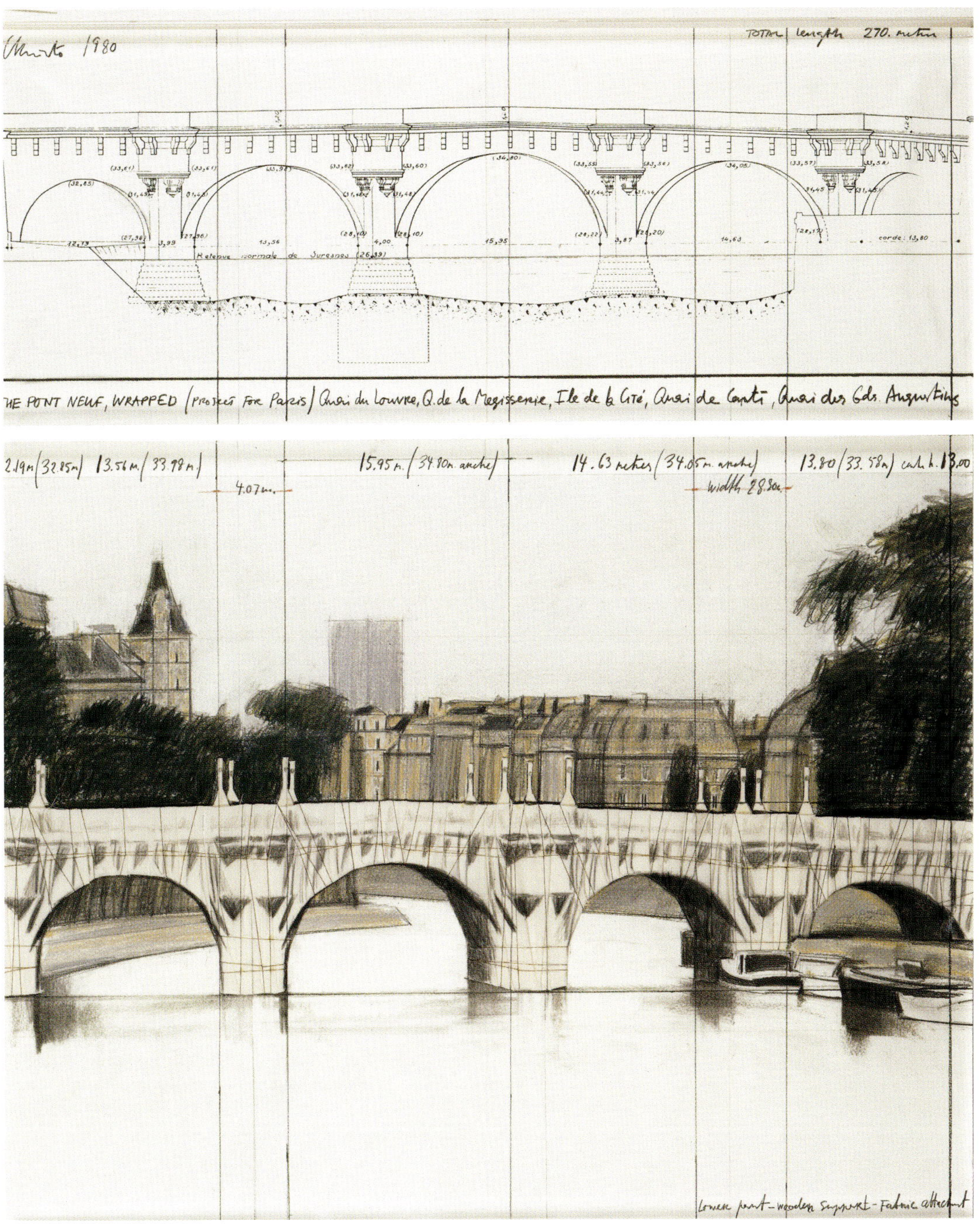
1980
TOTAL length 270. meters
HE PONT NEUF, WRAPPED (Project for Paris) Quai du Louvre, Q. de la Megisserie, Ile de la Cité, Quai de Conti, Quai des Gds. Augustins
15.95 m. (34.80m. arche)
14.63 meters (34.05 m. arche)
width 28.30m.
4.07m.
Lower part – wooden support – Fabric attachment

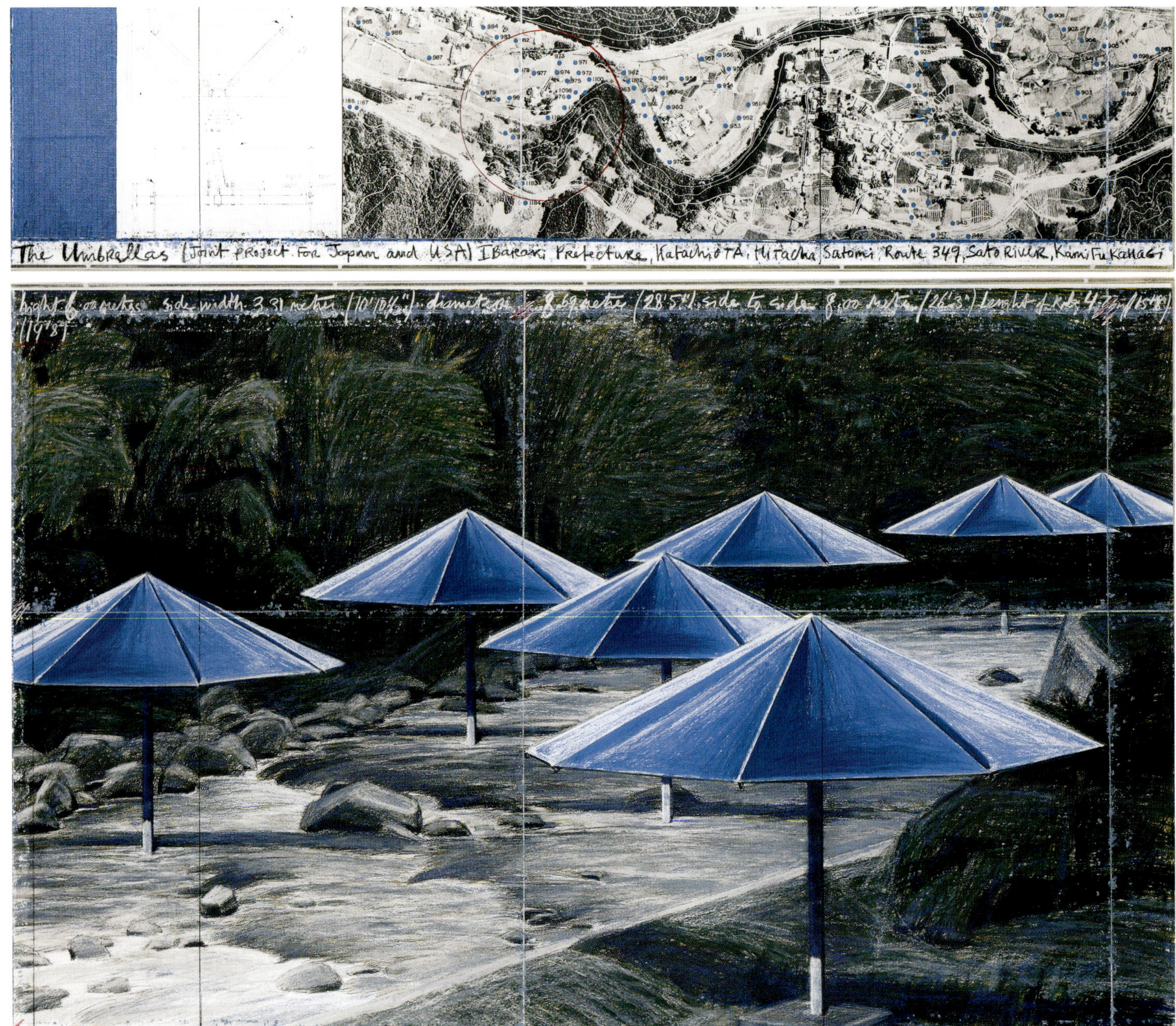
The Umbrellas (Joint Project for Japan and USA) Ibaraki Prefecture, Katachi OTA, Hitachi Satomi, Route 349, Sato River, Kami Fukanagi

THE UMBRELLAS, JAPAN – USA, 1984–1991

At sunrise, on October 9, 1991, Christo and Jeanne-Claude's 1,880 workers began to open the 3,100 umbrellas in Ibaraki and California, in the presence of the artists.

This Japan-USA temporary work of art reflected the similarities and differences in the ways of life and the use of the land in two inland valleys, one 12 miles (19 km) long in Japan, and the other 18 miles (29 km) long in the USA.

In Japan, the valley is located north of Hitachiota and south of Satomi, 75 miles (120 km) north of Tokyo, around Route 349 and the Sato River, in the Prefecture of Ibaraki, on the properties of 459 private landowners and governmental agencies.

In the U.S.A., the valley is located 60 miles (96.5 km) north of Los Angeles, along Interstate 5 and the Tejon Pass, between south of Gorman and Grapevine, on the properties of Tejon Ranch, 25 private landowners as well as governmental agencies.

Eleven manufacturers in Japan, USA, Germany and Canada prepared the various elements of *The Umbrellas*: fabric, aluminum super-structures, steel frame bases, anchors, wooden base supports, bags and molded base covers. All 3,100 umbrellas were assembled in Bakersfield, California, from where the 1,340 blue umbrellas were shipped to Japan.

Starting in December 1990, with a total work force of 500, Muto Construction Co. Ltd. in Ibaraki, and A. L. Huber & Son in California installed the earth anchors and steel bases. The sitting platform / base covers were placed during August and September 1991.

The Umbrellas, Joint Project for Japan and USA
Drawing (in two parts), 1991
15 x 65 in., 42 x 65 in.

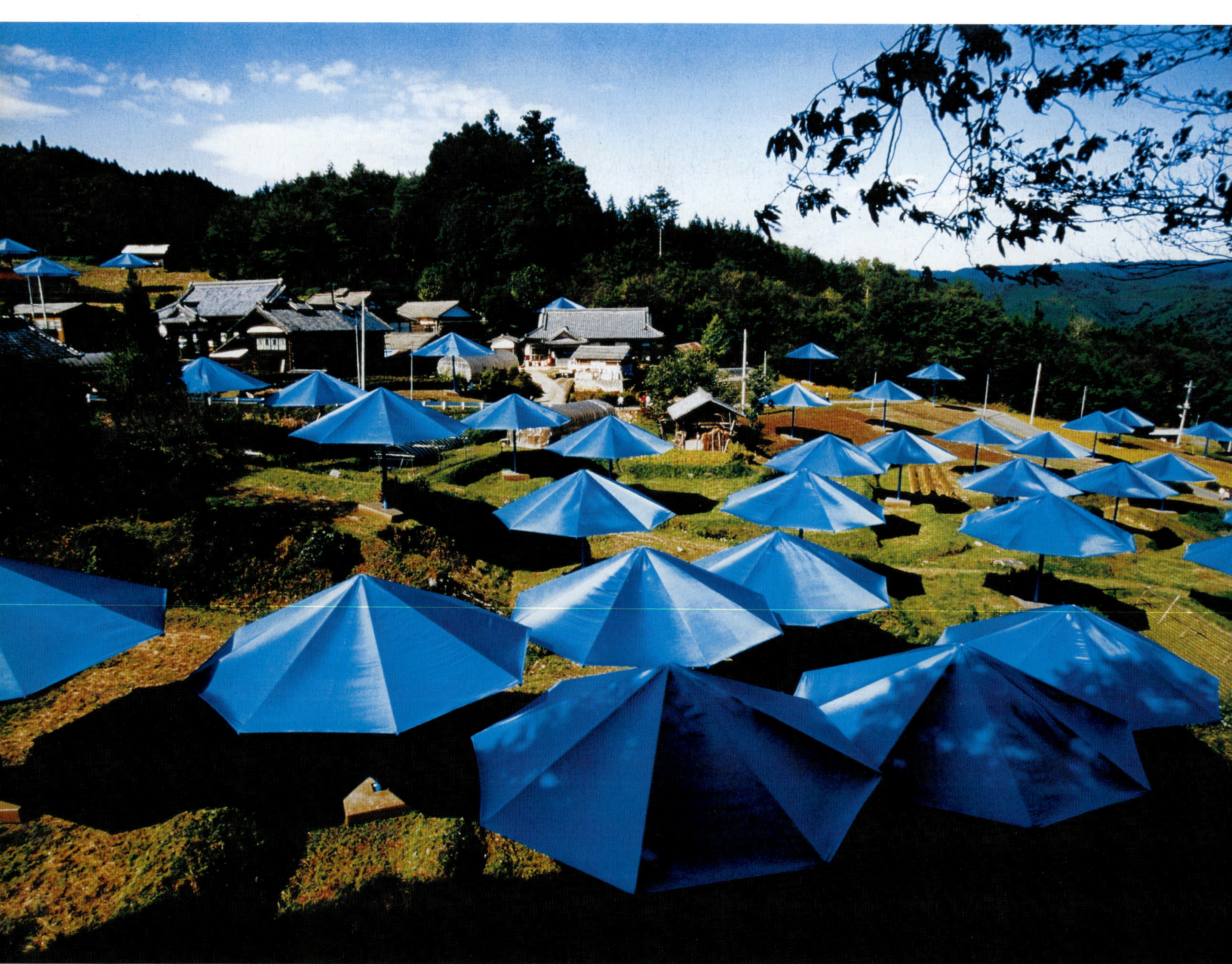

The Umbrellas (Japan site) 1984–1991
Photograph, 1991
28 x 39 ¾ in.
Photo: Wolfgang Volz

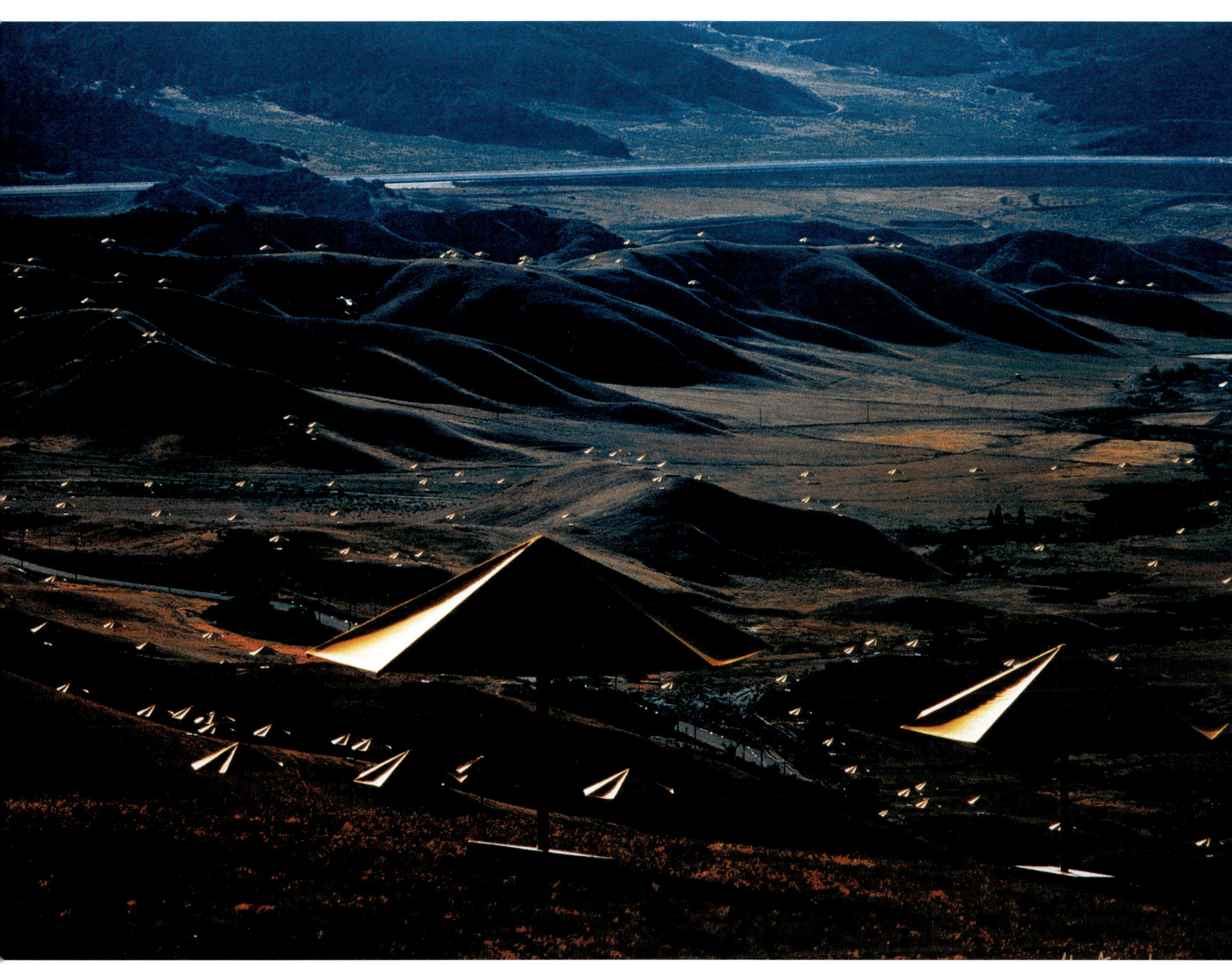

The Umbrellas, Japan and USA, 1984–1991
California, USA
Photograph, 1991
28 x 39 ¾ in.
Photo: Wolfgang Volz

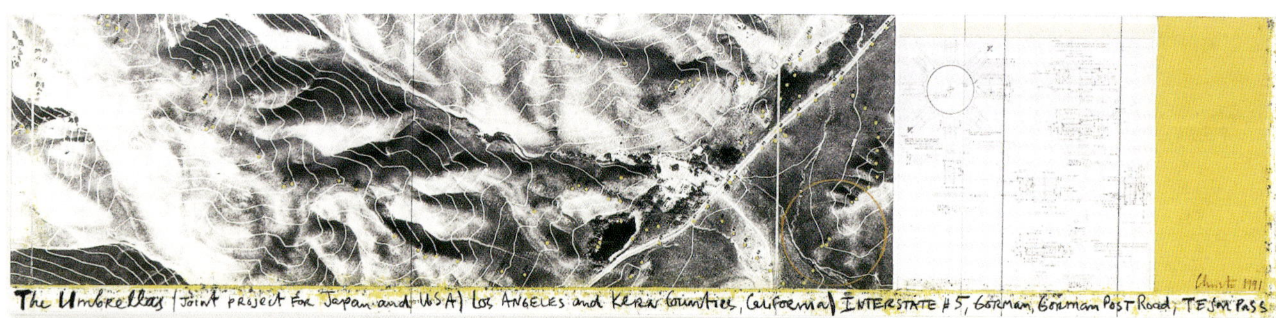

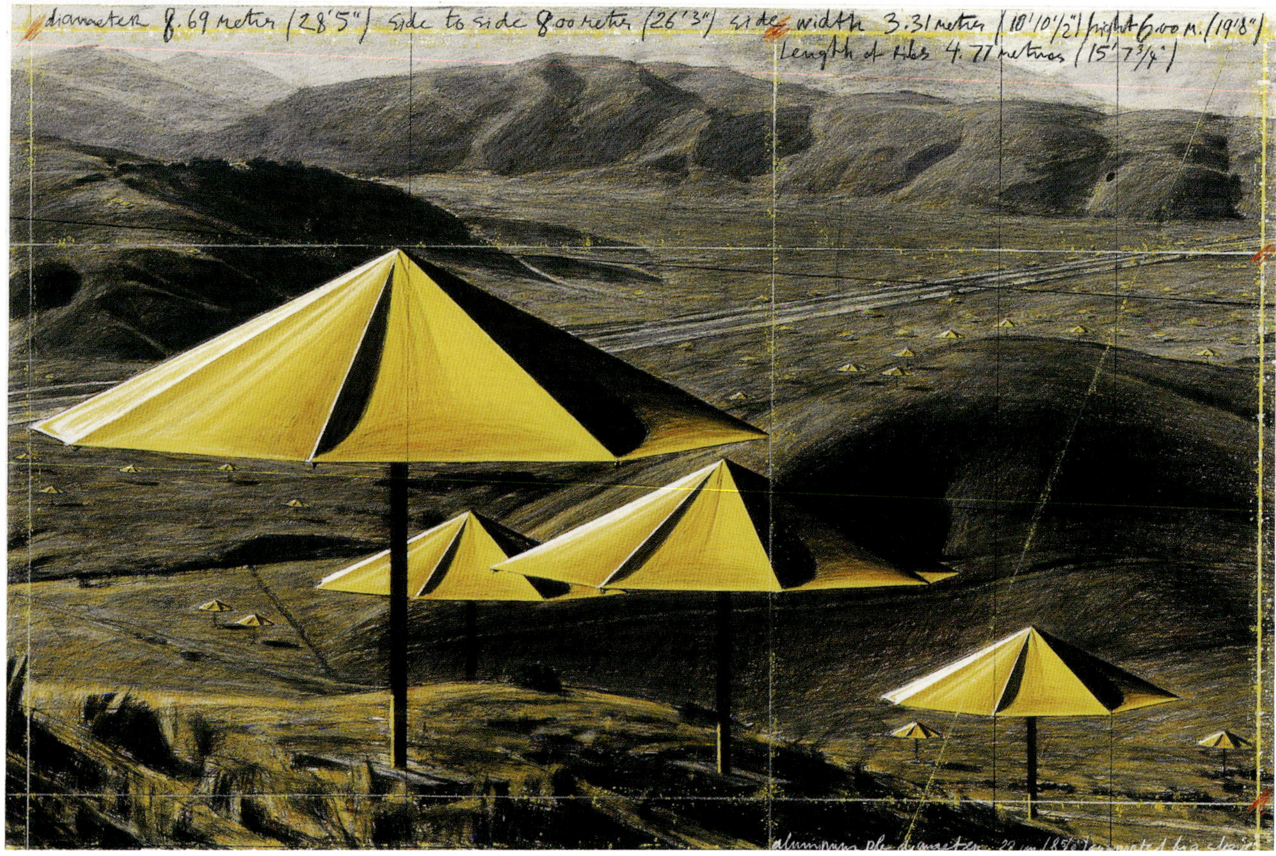

The Umbrellas, Joint Project for Japan and USA
Drawing in two parts, 1991
15 x 65 in., 42 x 65 in.

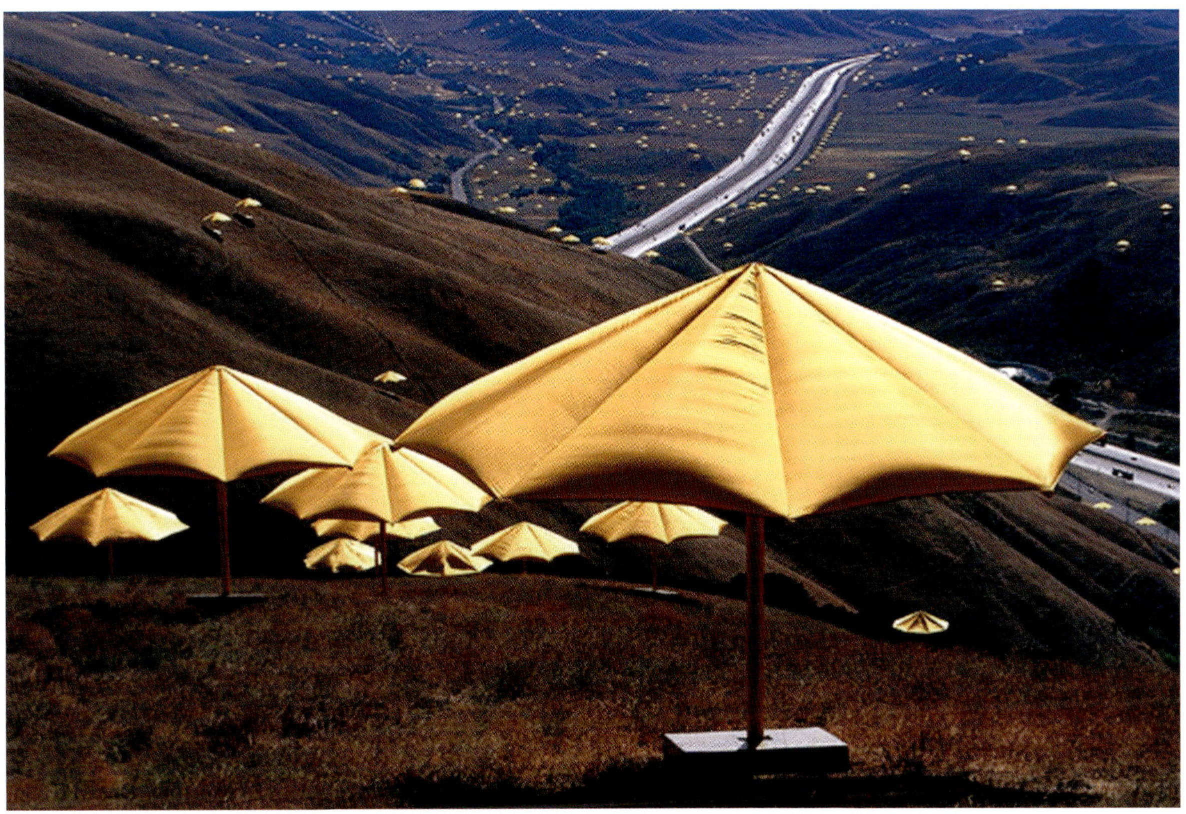

The Umbrellas, Japan and USA, 1984–1991
California, USA
Photo: Wolfgang Volz

From September 19 to October 7, 1991, an additional construction work force began transporting *The Umbrellas* to their assigned bases, bolted them to the receiving sleeves, and elevated the umbrellas to an upright closed position. On October 4, students, agricultural workers, and friends (960 in USA and 920 in Japan,) joined the work force to complete the installation of *The Umbrellas*. Each umbrella was 19 ft 8 in. high and 26 ft 5 in. in diameter.

The artists entirely financed their 26 million dollar temporary work of art through *The Umbrellas, Joint Project for Japan and U.S.A. Corporation* (Jeanne-Claude Christo-Javacheff, president). Previous projects by the artists have all been financed in a similar manner through the sale of the studies, preparatory drawings, collages, scale models, early works, and original lithographs. The artists do not accept any sponsorship.

The removal started on October 27 and the land was restored to its original condition. *The Umbrellas* were taken apart and all elements were recycled.

The Umbrellas, free standing dynamic modules, reflected the availability of the land in each valley, creating an invitational inner space, as houses without walls, or temporary settlements and related to the ephemeral character of the work of art. In the precious and limited space of Japan, *The Umbrellas* were positioned intimately, close together and sometimes following the geometry of the rice fields. In the luxuriant vegetation enriched by water year round, *The Umbrellas* were blue.

In the California vastness of uncultivated grazing land, the configuration of the umbrellas was whimsical and spreading in every direction. The brown hills are covered by blond grass, and in that dry landscape, *The Umbrellas* were yellow.

From October 9, 1991 for a period of 18 days, *The Umbrellas* were seen, approached, and enjoyed by the public, either by car from a distance and closer as they bordered the roads, or by walking under *The Umbrellas* in their luminous shadows.

Umbrellas:

How man in Japan (blue): 1340

How many in USA (yellow): 1760

Height including base: 19 ft 8 in.

Diameter of Umbrellas: 28 ft 5 in.

Weight of Umbrellas without base: 448 lb

Fabric area supported by Umbrella: 53.17 ft

Aluminum:

Diameter of Pole: 8.625 in.

Length of Ribs: 15 ft 7 in.

Size of Ribs: 3.75 x 2.25 in.

Length of Strut: 7 ft 5 in.

Diameter of Strut: 3 in.

Bases:

How many steel-bases in USA: 1625

How many concrete-bases in USA: 135

How many steel-bases in Japan: 1205

How many concrete-bases in Japan: 35

How many river-bases in Japan: 100

Totals for both Japan and U.S.A.:

Paint: 2,000 gallons

Total length Poles: 10.97 miles (17.7 km)

Total number of Ribs: 24,800

Total length Ribs: 73.5 miles (118.3 km)

Total number of Struts: 24,800

Total length Struts: 35 miles (56.3 km)

Total number of pieces per Umbrella: 470

Total number of pieces per steel-base with anchors: 64

Total number of all pieces: 1,655,400

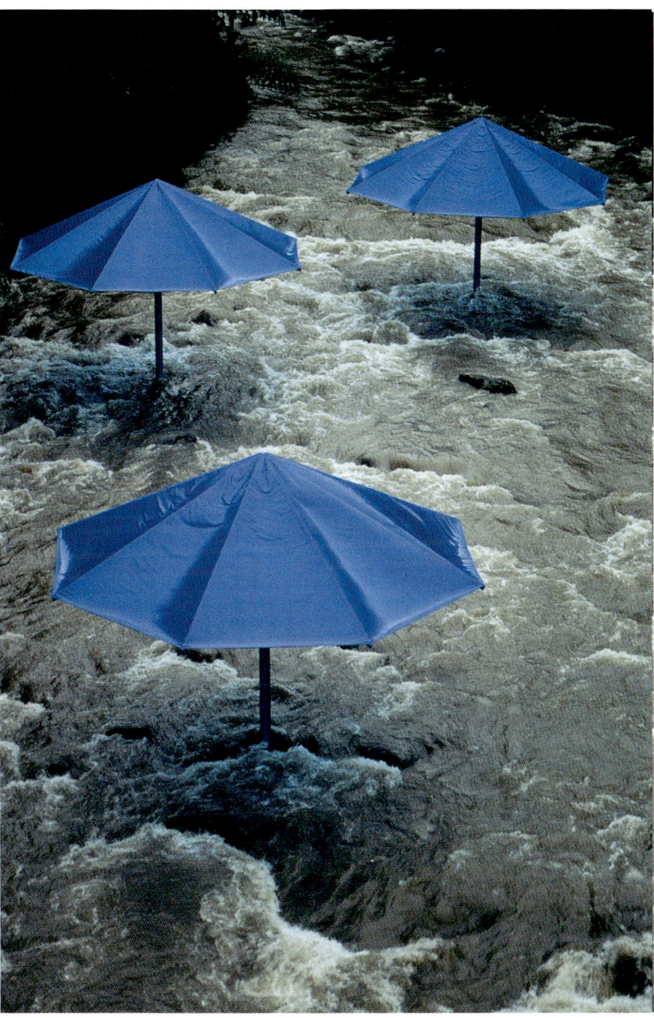

The Umbrellas, Japan and USA, 1984–1991
Ibaraki, Japan Site
Photo: Wolfgang Volz

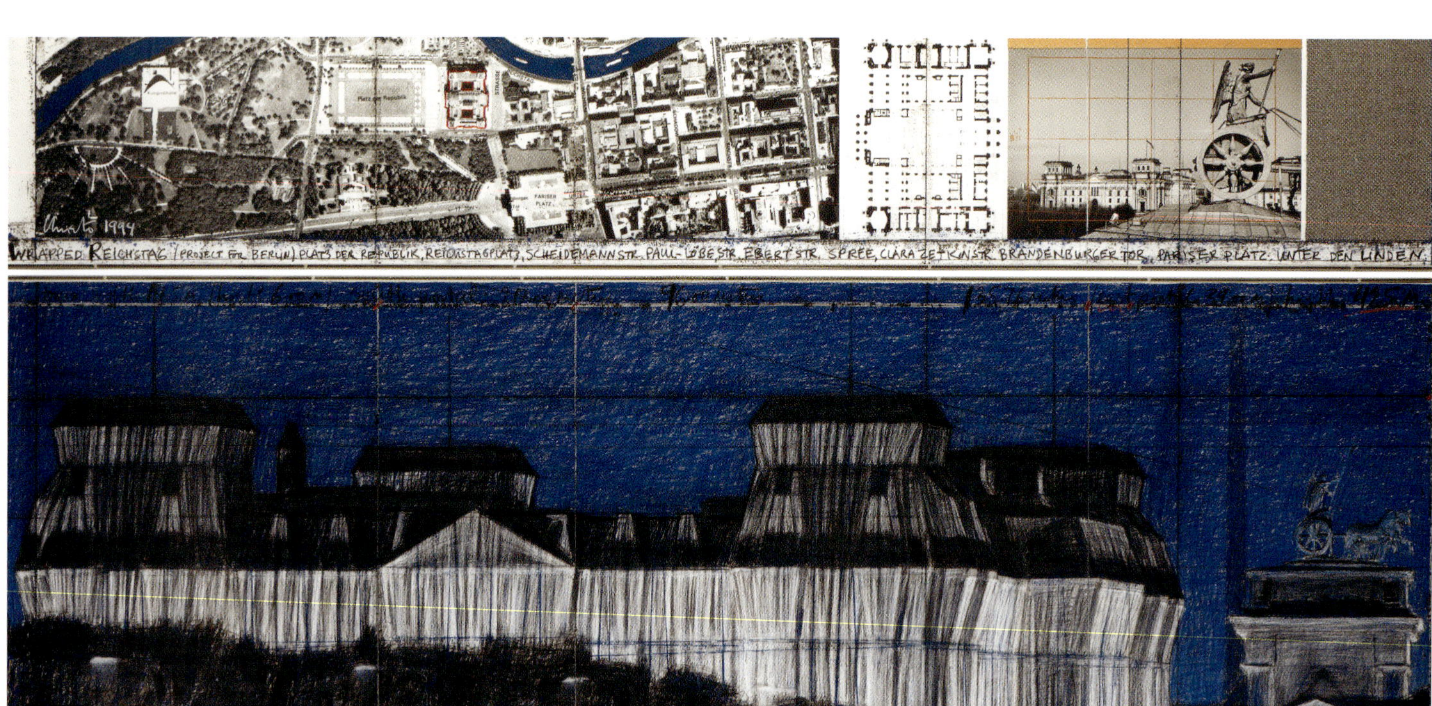

Wrapped Reichstag, Project for Berlin
Drawing (in two parts), 1994
15 x 96 in., 42 x 96 in.

WRAPPED REICHSTAG, Berlin 1971–1995

After a struggle spanning through the Seventies, Eighties and Nineties, the wrapping of the Reichstag was completed on June 24, 1995 by a work force of 90 professional climbers and 120 installation workers. The Reichstag remained wrapped for 14 days and all materials were recycled.

Ten companies in Germany started in September 1994 to manufacture all the various materials according to the specifications of the engineers. During the months of April, May, and June 1995, iron workers installed the steel structures on the towers, the roof, the statues and the stone vases to allow the folds of fabric to cascade from the roof down to the ground.

11,076,000 sq ft of thick woven polypropylene fabric with an aluminum surface and 51,181 ft of blue polypropylene rope, diameter 1.25 in., were used for the wrapping of the Reichstag. The facades, the towers and the roof were covered by 70 tailor-made fabric panels, twice as much fabric as the surface of the building.

The work of art was entirely financed by the artists, as have all their projects, through the sale of preparatory studies, drawings, collages, scale models as well as early works and original lithographs.

The artists do not accept sponsorship of any kind.

The *Wrapped Reichstag* represents not only 24 years of efforts in the lives of the artists but also years of team work by its leading members Michael S. Cullen, Wolfgang and Sylvia Volz, and Roland Specker. In Bonn, on February 25, 1994, at a plenary session, presided by Prof. Dr. Rita Süssmuth, the German

Bundestag (parliament) debated for 70 minutes and voted on the work of art. The result of the roll call vote was: 292 in favor, 223 against and nine abstentions.

The Reichstag stands up in an open, strangely metaphysical area, The building has experienced its own continuous changes and perturbations: built in 1894, burned in 1933, almost destroyed in 1945, it was restored in the sixties, but the Reichstag always remained the symbol of Democracy.

Throughout the history of art, the use of fabric has been a fascination for artists. From the most ancient times to the present, fabric, forming folds, pleats and draperies, is a significant part of paintings, frescoes, reliefs and sculptures made of wood, stone and bronze. The use of fabric on the Reichstag follows the classical tradition. Fabric, like clothing or skin, is fragile, it translates the unique quality of impermanence.

For a period of two weeks, the richness of the silvery fabric, shaped by the blue ropes, created a sumptuous flow of vertical folds highlighting the features and proportions of the imposing structure, revealing the essence of the Reichstag.

FACT SHEET
Christo and Jeanne-Claude: Wrapped Reichstag, Berlin 1971–1995

The Building: The German Reichstag
Height at roof: 105.5 ft
Height at towers: 139.4 ft
Length, East and West facade: 445.2 ft
Width, North and South facade: 314.9 ft

Total perimeter: 1,520.3 ft
Number of towers: 4
Numberof inner courtyards: 2

The Materials
Length of yarn used for weaving: 48,836 miles (70,546 km)
Manufactured by Bremer Woll-Kammerei, Bremen, Germany

Silver polypropylene fabric (fire-retardant B1): 119,603 sq yds
Woven by Schilgen, Emsdetten, Germany
Width of the original woven fabric: 5 ft
Tensile strength of fabric: 4000 Newtons per 2 in.
Total weight of fabric: 135,582 lb
Weight of aluminum for metallization for 40 in.: 8.82 lb
metallized by Rowo-Coating, Herbolzheim, Germany

Fabric panels: 70
Sewn by Spreewald Planen, Vetschau, Germany and
Zeltaplan Taucha, Germany and Canobbio, Castelnuovo, Italy
Average size of panel: 121.4 ft x 131.2 ft
Length of sewing thread: 807.8 miles (1,300 km)
Total length of all seams: 568,678 yds
Blue propylene rope with a diameter of ¾ of an inch: 17,060 yds
manufactured by Gleistein, Bremen, Germany

Window-anchors: 110
Roof-anchors: 270
Weight of steel for roof: 440,917 lb
Weight of steel for window-anchors: 77,160 lb

Cages for statues: 16

Size of cages for statues: 31.2 ft x 16.4 ft x 14.7 ft

All steel manufactured by Stahlbau Zwickau, Zwickau, Germany

Air-cushions (necessary during installation): 32

Manufactured by Heba, Emsdetten, Germany

FACT SHEET

Christo and Jeanne-Claude: Wrapped Reichstag, Berlin 1971–1995

Number of weights on ground, attached to fabric: 477 (1.5 tons per meter)

manufactured by EKO Stahl, Eisenhuttenstadt, Germany

Total weight on ground: 2,205,000 lb

The Work Force

Chief executive officers: Roland Specker (administration) and Wolfgang Volz (technical and construction)

Engineering planning: IPL Ingenieurplanung Leichtbau, Radolfzell, Germany

Engineering advisors: Vince Davenport, John Thompson, Dimeter Zagoroff

Crew to install the fabric and the ropes: RVM, Berlin headed by Frank Seltenheim

Exclusive photographers: Wolfgang and Sylvia Volz

Monitor organization: Siegward Hausmann under the guidance of Simon Chaput

Number of monitors: 1200 (in 2 periods)

600 in four 6-hour shifts of 150 monitors each

Number of professional climbers: 90 (in 2 shifts of 45 each)

Number of installation workers: 120 (in 2 shifts of 60 each)

Number of office staff in Berlin: 17

Number of office staff in New York: (Calixte Stamp and Vladimir Yavachev)

Legal Background:

The project is being carried out by Verhullter Reichstag GmbH, a subsidiary of C.V.J. Corporation, Jeanne-Claude

Christo-Javacheff, President and Treasurer, Scott Hodes, Secretary and Leal Counsel, Christo V. Javacheff, Assistant Secretary. Legal counsel is provided by attorneys Prof. Dr. Peter Raue and Scott Hodes. Architectural advice is provided by Prof. Jurgen Sawade. Historical advice is provided by Michael S. Cullen. Permits were required and recieved from the German Parliament, the Bundestag, and from the local administration in Berlin, the city district department Tiergarten and all concerned agencies.

Number of visits by the Christos to Germany: 54 (1976–1995)
Members of parliament visited: 352
Number of presidents of the Bundestag (German Parliament) involved: 6 (1976–1995)

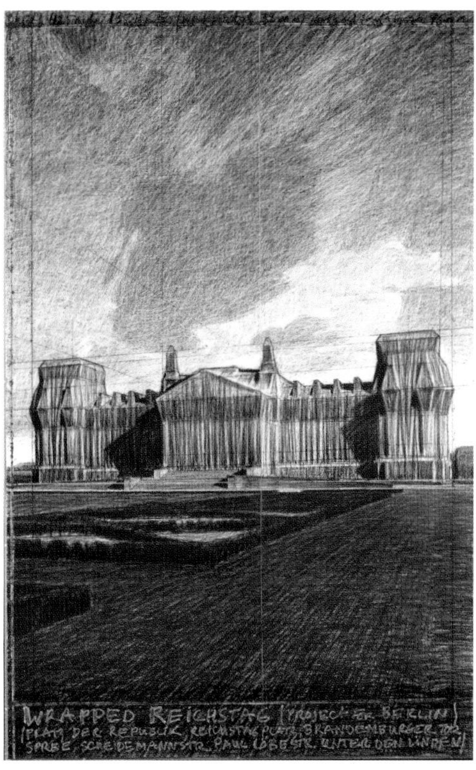

Wrapped Reichstag, Project for Berlin
Drawing, 1994
65 x 42 in.

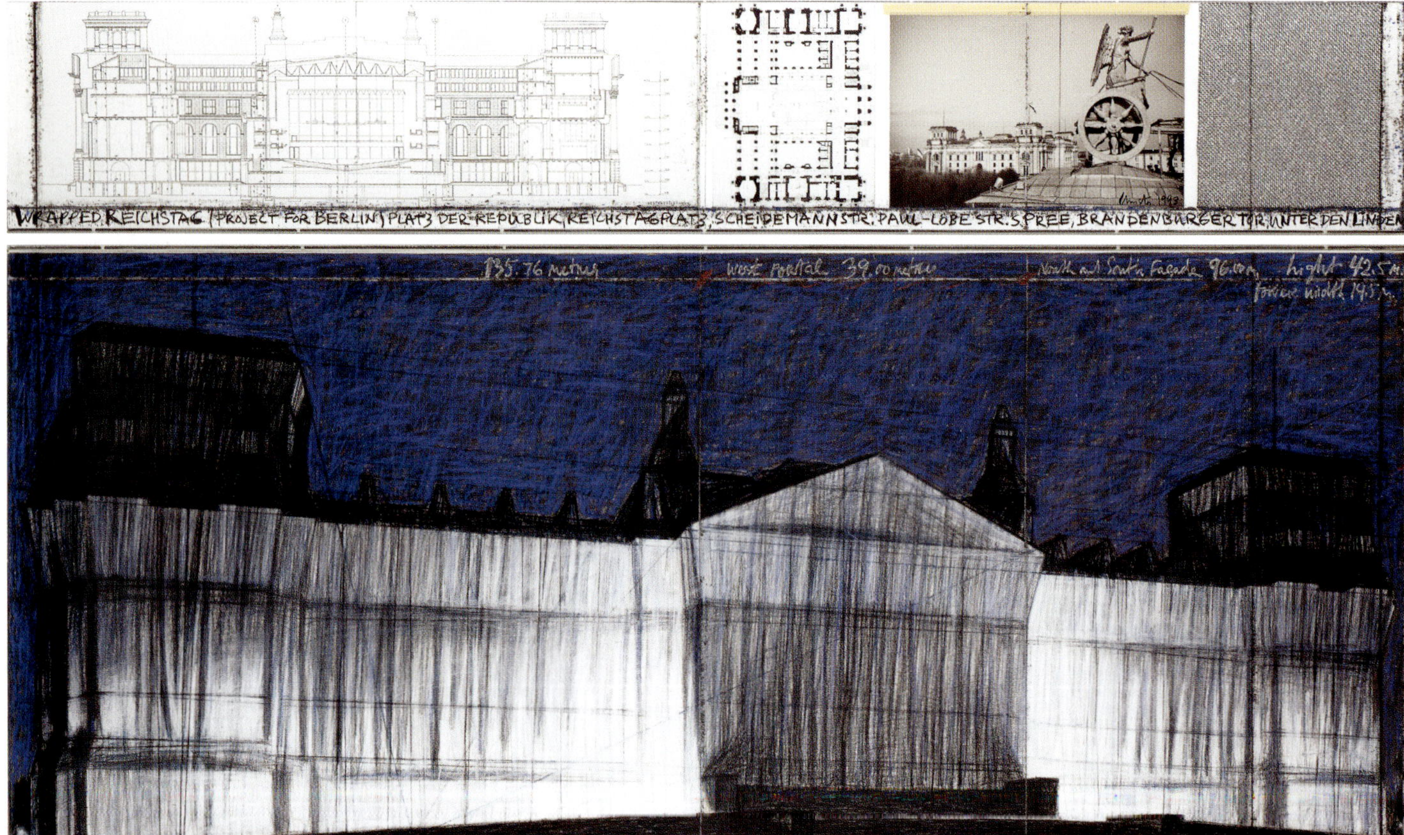

Wrapped Reichstag, Project for Berlin
Drawing (in two parts), 1993
15 x 96 in., 42 x 96 in.

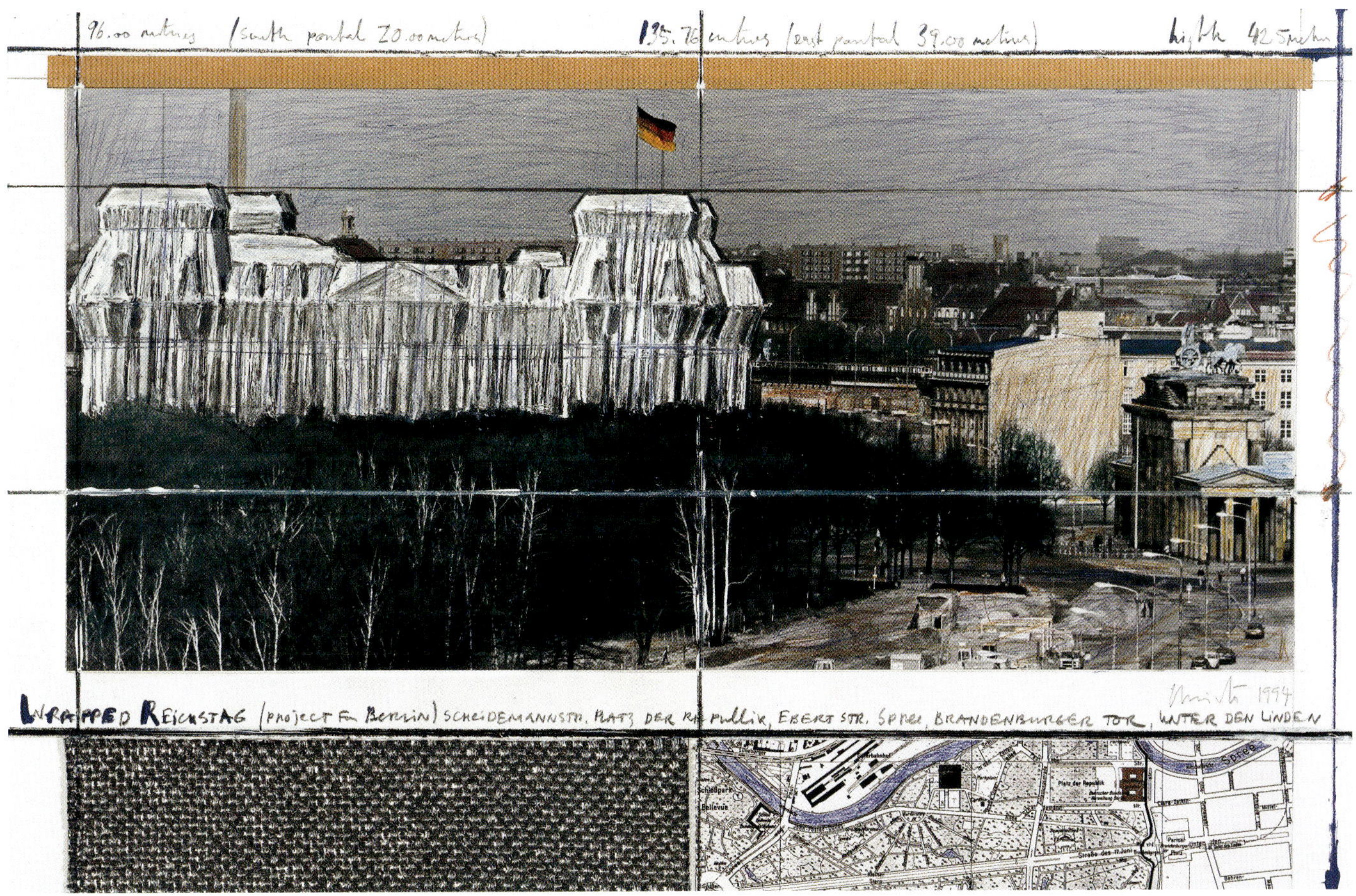

Wrapped Reichstag, Project for Berlin
Collage, 1994
14 x 22 in.

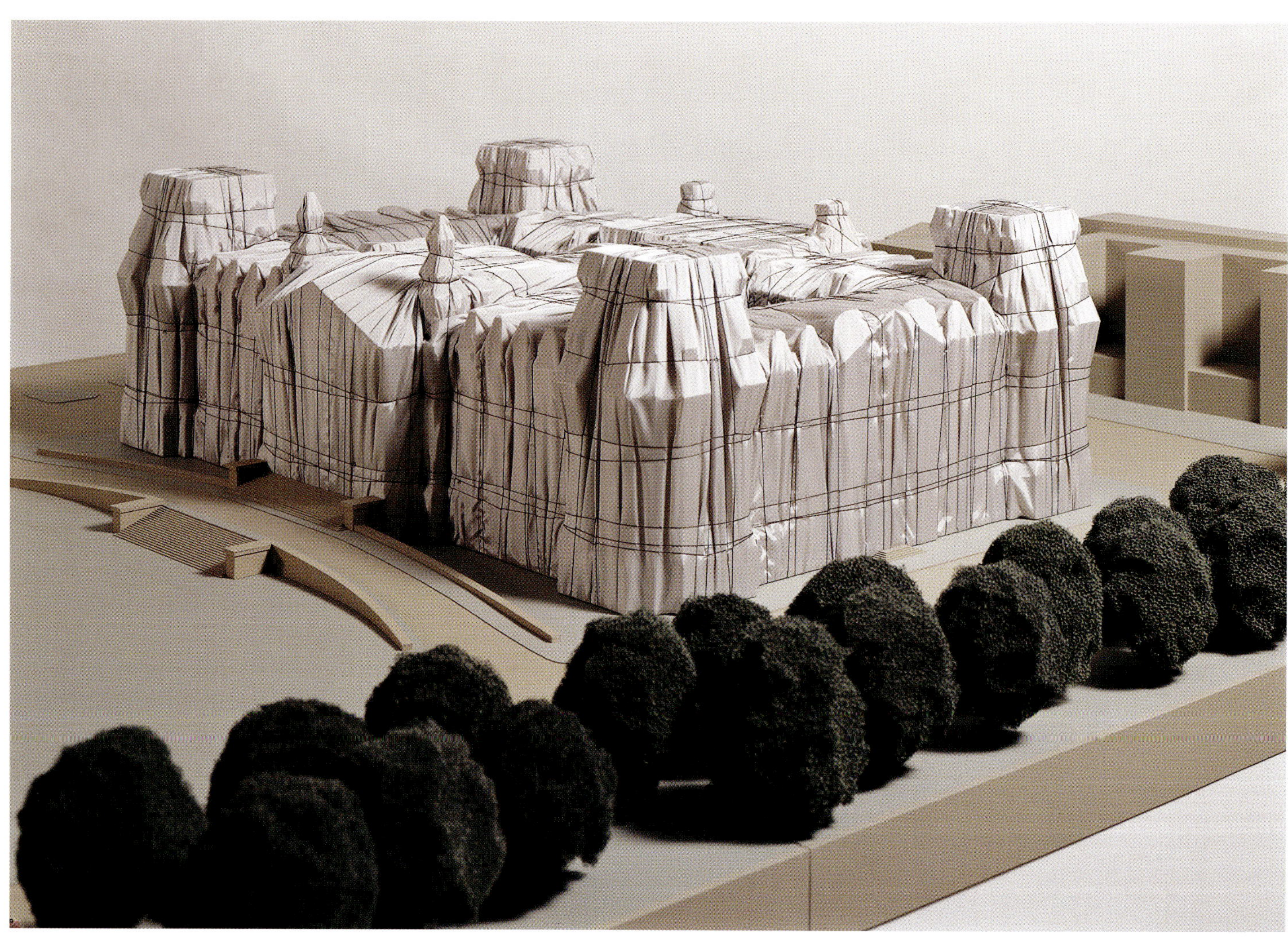

Wrapped Reichstag, Project for Berlin
Scale model, 1993
31 ½ x 98 ½ x 197 in.
Photo: Wolfgang Volz

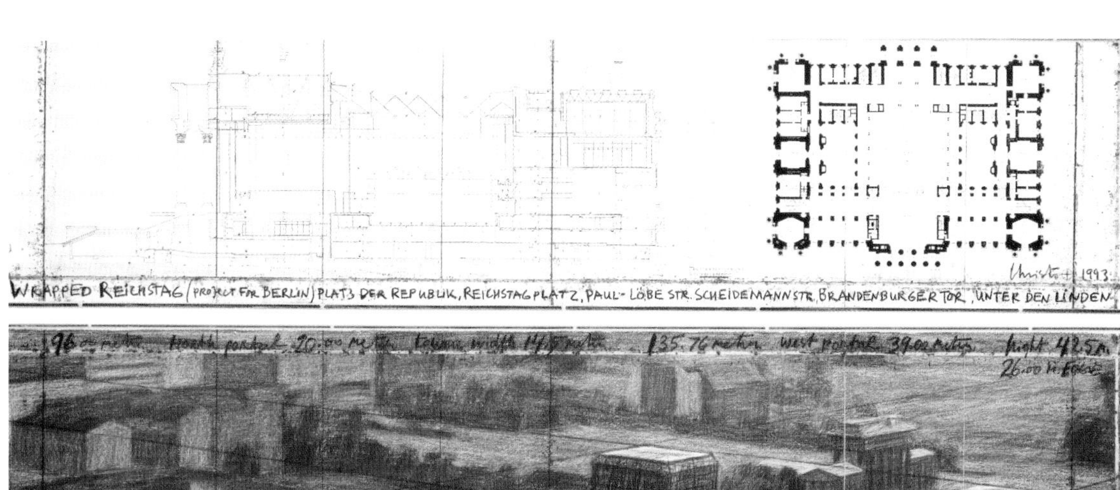

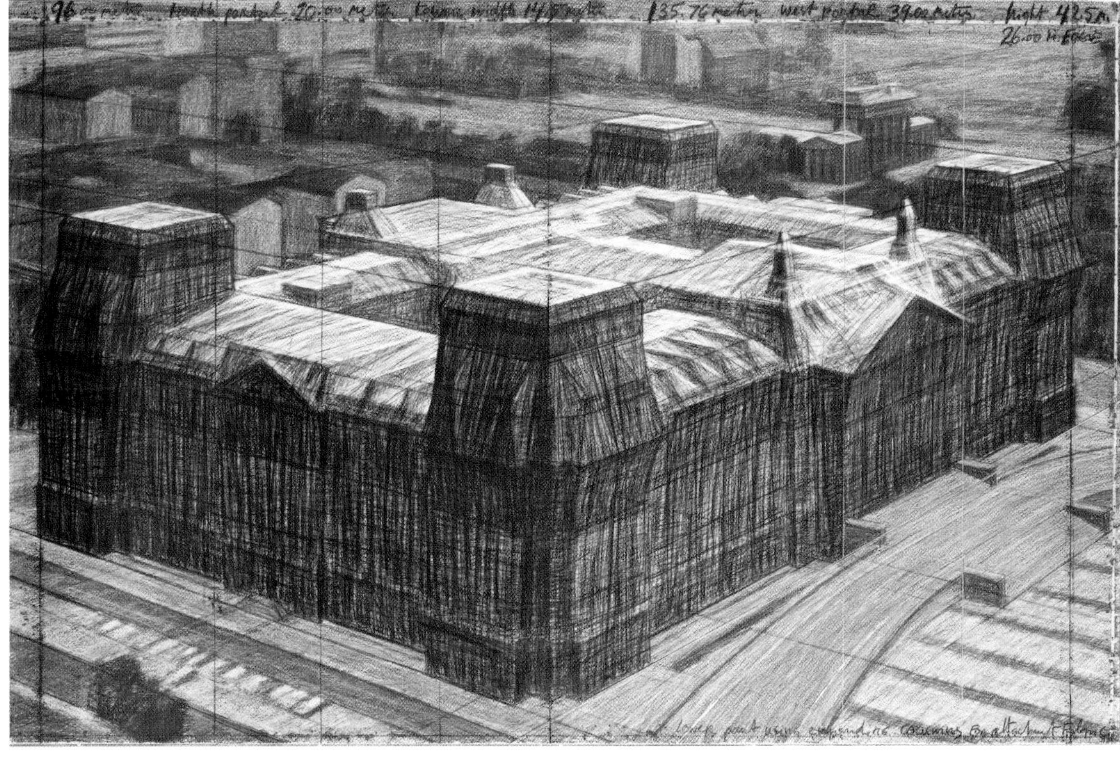

Wrapped Reichstag, Project for Berlin
Drawing (in two parts)
1993
15 x 65 in., 42 x 65 in.

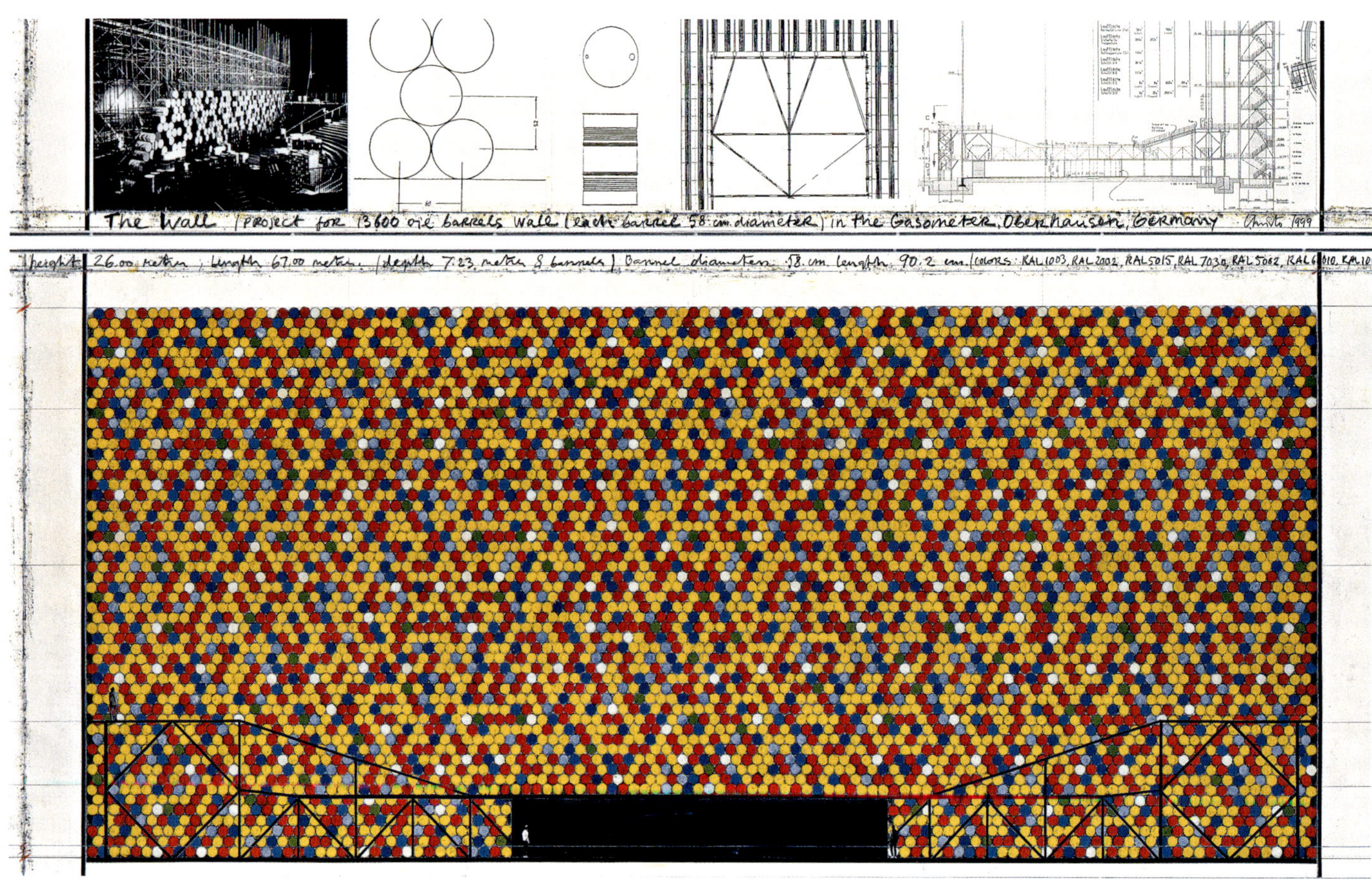
The Wall (Project for 13600 oil barrels Wall (each barrel 58 cm diameter) in the Gasometer, Oberhausen, Germany
Christo 1999
height 26.00 meter; length 67.00 meter (depth 7.23 meter 8 barrels) Barrel diameter 58 cm length 90.2 cm (colors: RAL 1003, RAL 2002, RAL 5015, RAL 7030, RAL 5002, RAL 6010, RAL 10

THE WALL, 13,000 Oil Barrels, Gasometer, Oberhausen, Germany 1999

Christo and Jeanne-Claude have created an installation and premiere two exhibitions of documentation inside the Gasometer. It opened on May 1,1999 in Oberhausen, Germany. The works remained until mid-October 1999.

The Gasometer is one of the largest tank structures in the world. It was built in 1928 to store the gaseous by-products of iron ore processing. The Gasometer has recently been used as exhibit and event space. The round structure is 110 m (360 ft) high by 68 m (223 ft) in diameter.

Christo and Jeanne-Claude's installation is:

THE WALL, 13,000 OIL BARRELS

The Wall bisects the Gasometer into two halves. The oil barrel structure is 26 m (85 ft) tall and 68 m (223 ft) wide with a depth of 7.23 m (24 ft).

Sharing the Gasometer with the installation is the first public exhibition of documentation of:

The Umbrellas, Japan-USA, 1984–1991 Documentation Exhibition
Wrapped Reichstag, Berlin, 1971–1995 Documentation Exhibition

The use of oil barrels follows a tradition in the work of Christo and Jeanne-Claude including:

The two exhibitions showed the chronology of Christo and Jeanne-Claude's temporary works of art from their conception to their completion. They included original preparatory drawings, collages, scale models, and examples of the materials used in the projects: steel, aluminum, fabric and rope, technical, engineering and legal documents, as well as a large number of color and black and white photographs of the negotiations, installation and completion.

The construction of *The Wall* was organized by Wolfgang Volz.

The IBA Emscher Park Organization was founded by the state of North Rhine, Westfalia in 1989 to improve the infrastructure of the Ruhrgebiet. That organization's last act was its invitation to Christo and Jeanne-Claude to install: The Wall, 13,600 Oil Barrels and the two documentation exhibitions: The Umbrellas, Japan-USA, 1984–1991 and Wrapped Reichstag, Berlin, 1971–1995.

The installation and exhibit transformed the already unusual space of the Gasometer, providing new ways of experiencing its form and viewers' participation with it.

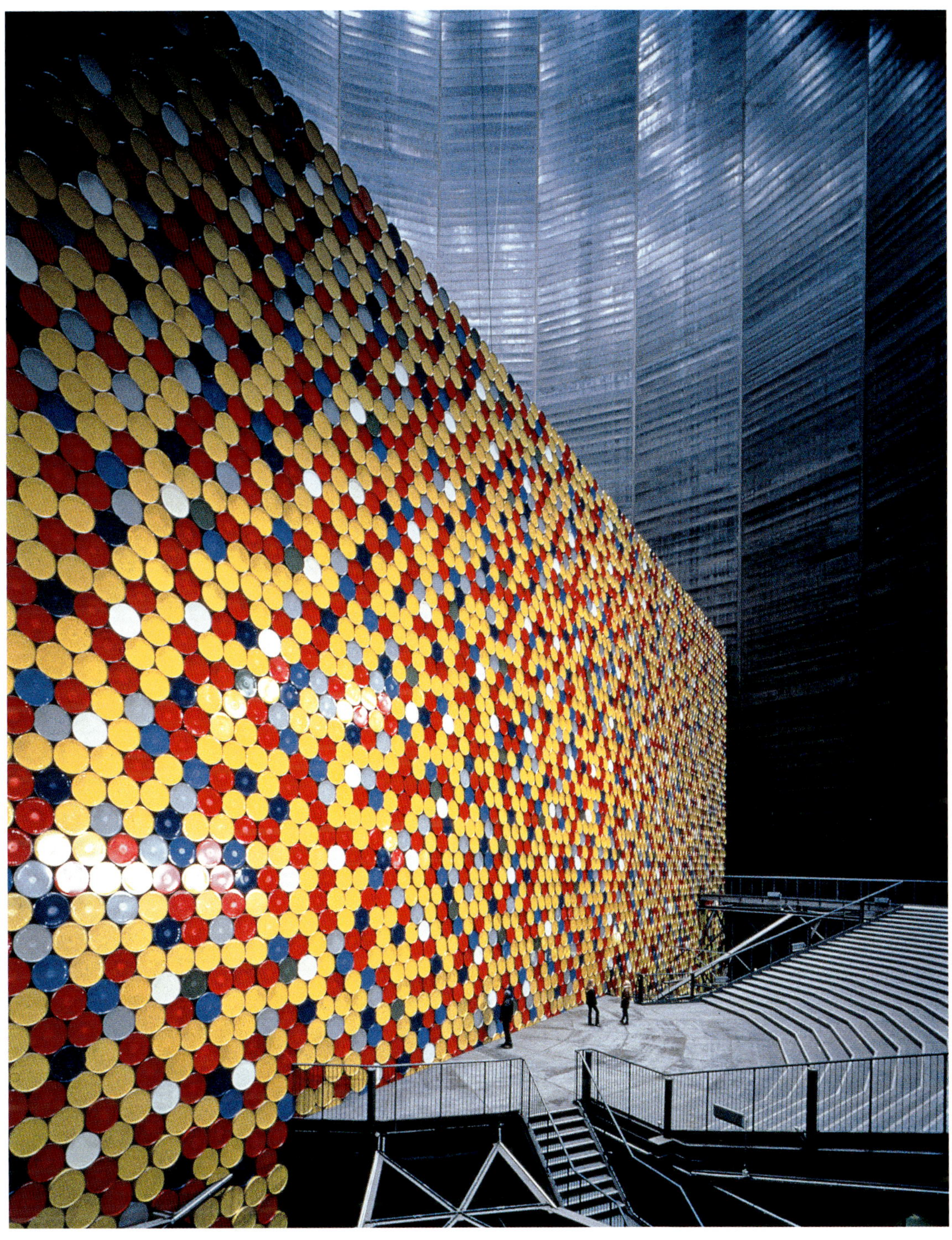

The Wall: 13,000 Oil Barrels, Oberhausen, Gasometer, Germany, 1999
30 ½ x 27 ¾ in.
Photo: Wolfgang Volz

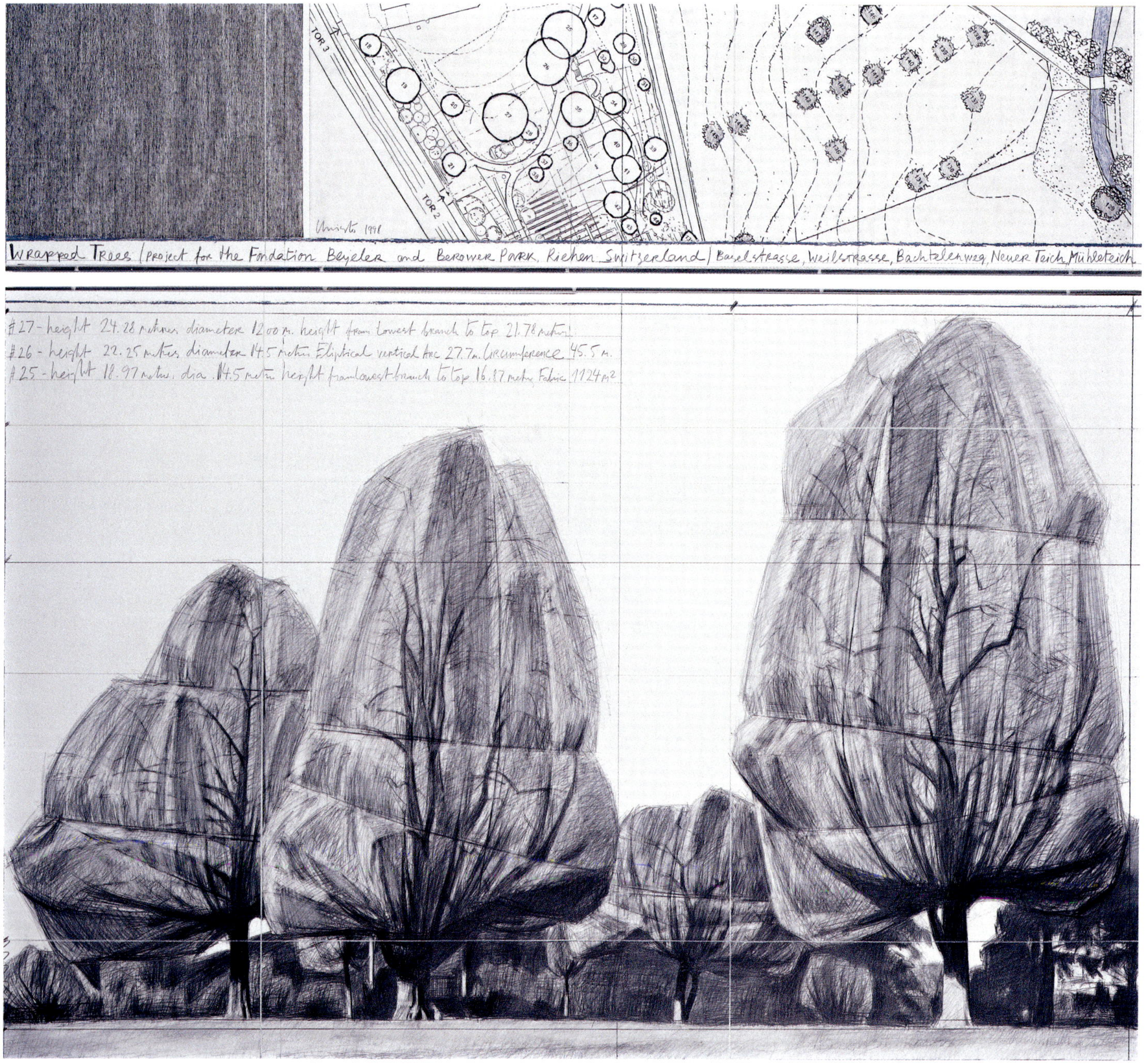

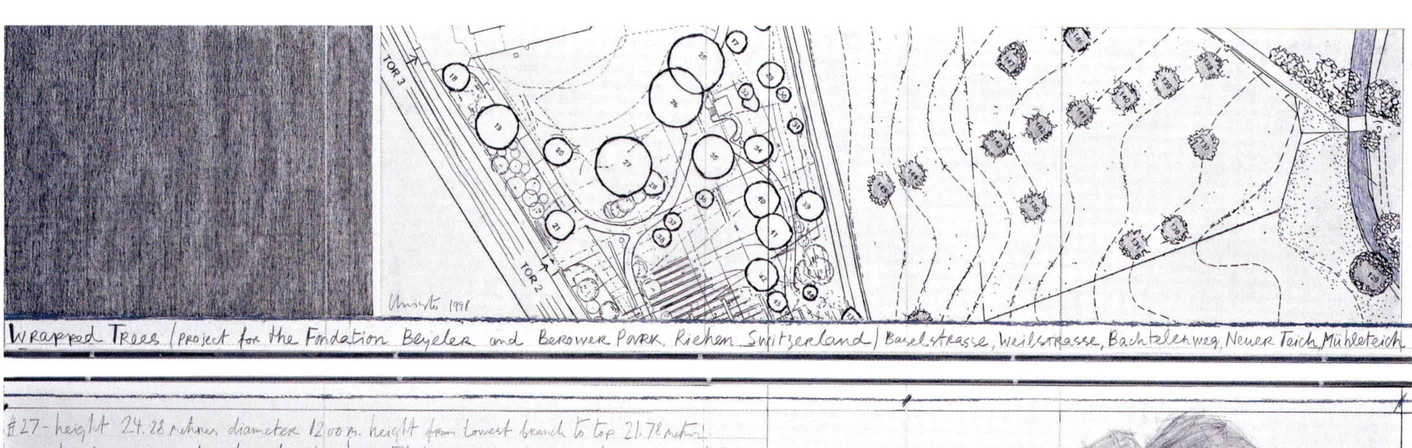

Wrapped Trees: Project for Fondation Beyeler and Berower Park, Riehen, Switzerland, 1997–1998
Drawing (in two parts), 1998
15 x 65 in., 42 x 65 in.

WRAPPED TREES, Fondation Beyeler and Berower Park, Riehen, Switzerland, 1997–1998

Starting on Friday, November 13, 1998, 178 trees were wrapped with 592,034 sq ft of woven polyester fabric (used every winter in Japan to protect the trees from frost and heavy snow) and 14.35 miles (23.1 km) of rope.

The trees are located in the park around the Fondation Beyeler and in the adjacent meadow as well as along the creek of Berower Park. The first record of Berower Park goes back to the year 1551. A 1786 map of Riehen shows a small French garden and a large area of vineyards. In 1832 it was redesigned by F. R. Caillat as a privately owned English park.

In 1976 the ownership of Berower Park was transferred to the community of Riehen, located north-east of Basel, at the border of Germany. The park includes a great diversity of trees: Chestnut, Oak, Ash, Plum, Cherry, Linden, Gingko, Beech, Birch, Sycamore, Maple, Catalpa, Hazelnut and Golden Weeping Willow. The height of the trees varies between 82 ft and 6.56 ft with a diameter from 47 ft to 3.25 ft.

The project was organized by Josy Kraft, project director and by Wolfgang and Sylvia Volz, project managers, who also surveyed the trees and designed the sewing patterns for each tree.

J. Schilgen GmbH & Co., Emsdetten, Germany wove the fabric. Günter Heckmann, Emsdetten, Germany cut and sewed the fabric according to each pattern. Meister + Cie. AG, Hasle-Rüegsau, Switzerland manufactured the ropes.

Field manager Frank Seltenheim of Seilpartner, Berlin, Germany, directed eight teams working simultaneously: ten climbers, three tree pruners and 20 workers.

As they have always done, Christo and Jeanne-Claude have paid the expenses of the project themselves through the sale of original works to museums, private collectors and galleries.

Before the leaves start growing again the wrapping will be removed and the materials will be recycled.

Christo and Jeanne-Claude have worked with trees for many years: in 1966 a 33 ft long Wrapped Tree was part of a personal exhibition at the Stedelijk van AbbeMuseum in Eindhoven, Holland, and Wrapped Trees was proposed for the park adjacent to the Saint Louis Museum of Art, Missouri. In 1968, at the occasion of a personal exhibition at the Museum of Modern Art in New York, there was a project for Wrapped Trees for the museum's garden. In 1969, Two Wrapped Trees 31 ft and 17 ft were created in Sydney, Australia for the art collector John Kaldor. Also in 1969, the artists requested permission for Wrapped Trees, Project for 330 Trees, Avenue des Champs-Elysées, Paris which was denied by Maurice Papon, Prefect of Paris.

The Wrapped Trees in Riehen are the outcome of 32 years of effort.

On November 13, 1998, an exhibition opened at the Galerie Beyeler in Basel, retracing the itinerary of those proposals with collages, drawings and scale models created through the years and preparatory studies for the Wrapped Trees in Riehen as well as some early works of the fifties and sixties.
An historical exhibition from Cézanne to modern masters and contemporary artists, Magic of Trees is being held at the Fondation Beyeler.

The branches of the Wrapped Trees pushing the translucent fabric outward create dynamic volumes of light and shadow, moving in the wind with new forms and surfaces shaped by the ropes on the fabric.

PRESS COMMINQUE
Christo & Jeanne-Claude

Riehen, Switzerland, December 3, 1998

"We have seen our work of art, Wrapped Trees, Fondation Beyeler and Berower Park, 1997–1998, as part of the exhibition The Magic of Trees at the Fondation Beyeler. Together with the Fondation, we had planned that the Wrapped Trees might remain longer than the usual 14 days.

However, as with all of previous temporary work of art, the 14 day duration of the project's exhibition has been an aesthetic choice.

Therefore, after having enjoyed and shared our work of art with so many visitors, as artists, we have now decided that Wrapped Trees, Fondation Beyeler and Berower Park, 1997–1998 will remain until December 13, 1998. Then the project will be removed and all materials will be recycled.

Statement
The temporality of a work of art creates a feeling of fragility, vulnerability and an urgency to be seen, as well as a presence of the missing, because we know it will be gone tomorrow.

The quality of love and tenderness that human beings have towards what will not last – for instance the love and tenderness we have for childhood and our lives - is a quality we want to give to our work as an additional aesthetic quality".

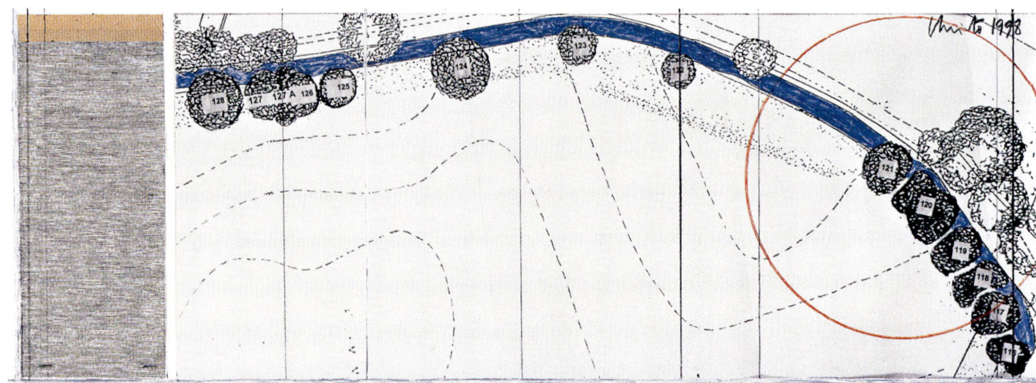

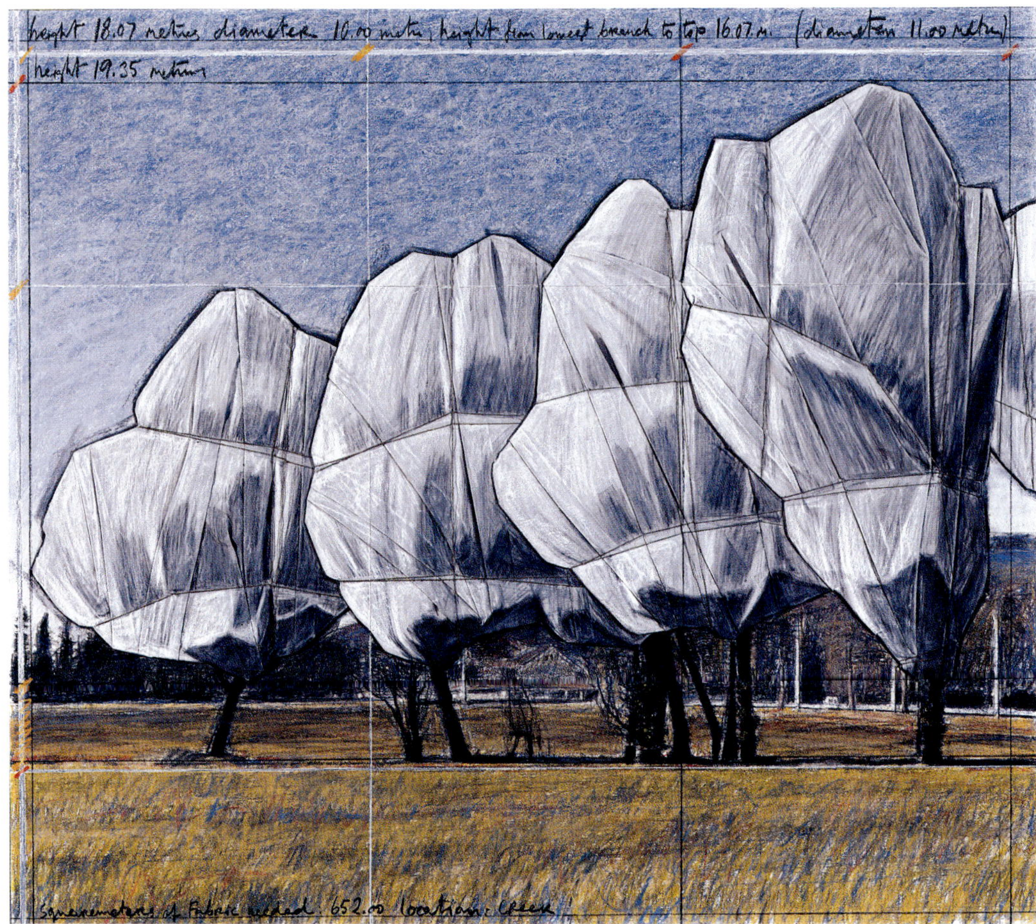

Wrapped Trees: Project for Fondation Beyeler and Berower Park, Riehen
Collage (in two parts), 1998
12 x 30 ½ in., 26 ¼ x 30 ½ in.

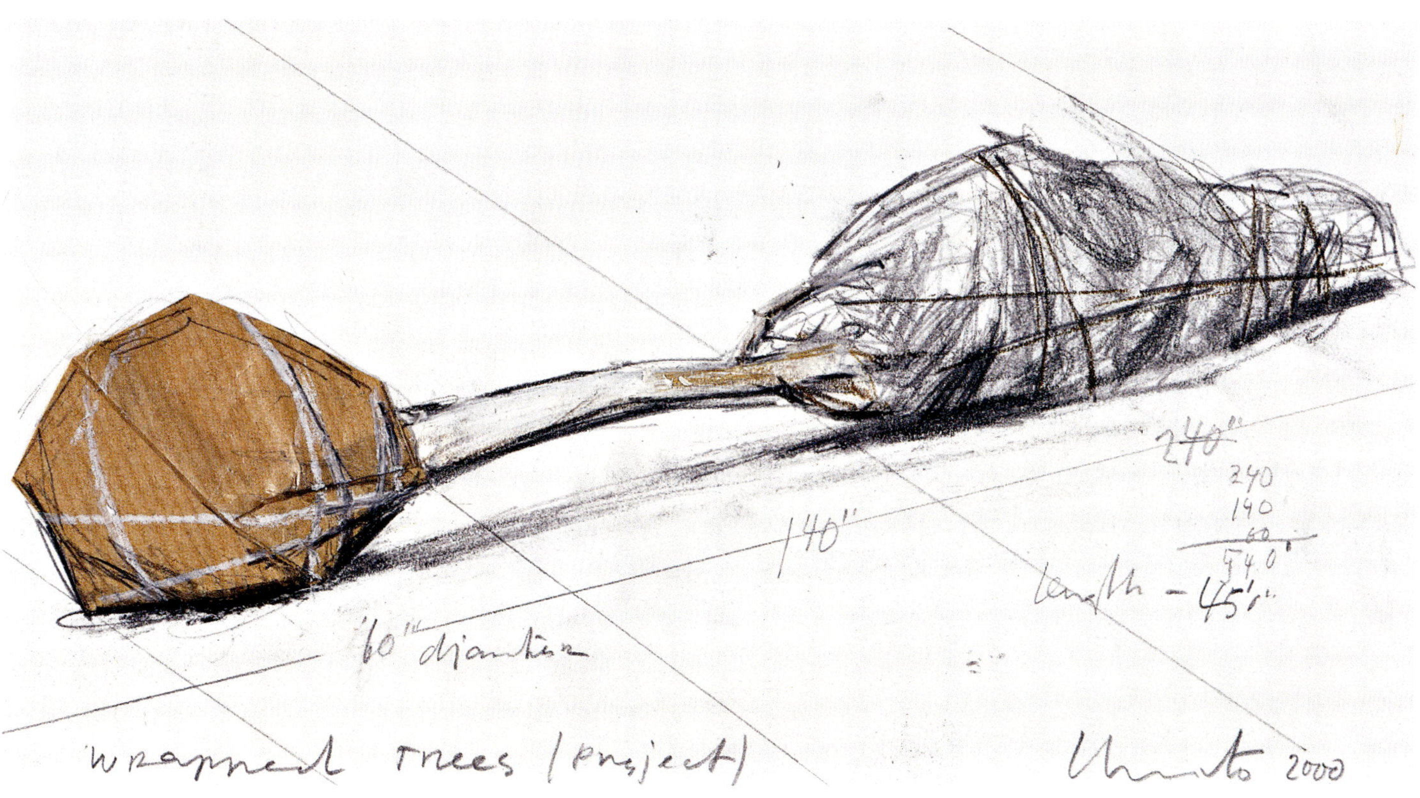

Wrapped Tree (Project)
Collage, 2000
4 ¾ x 8 ⅞ in.

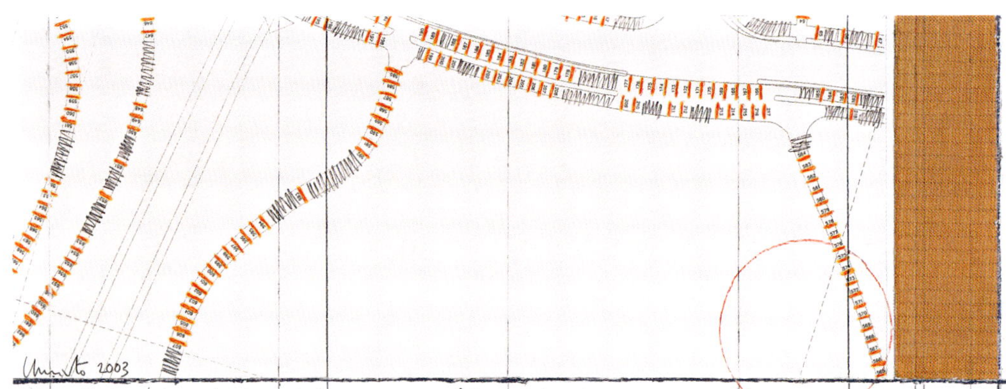

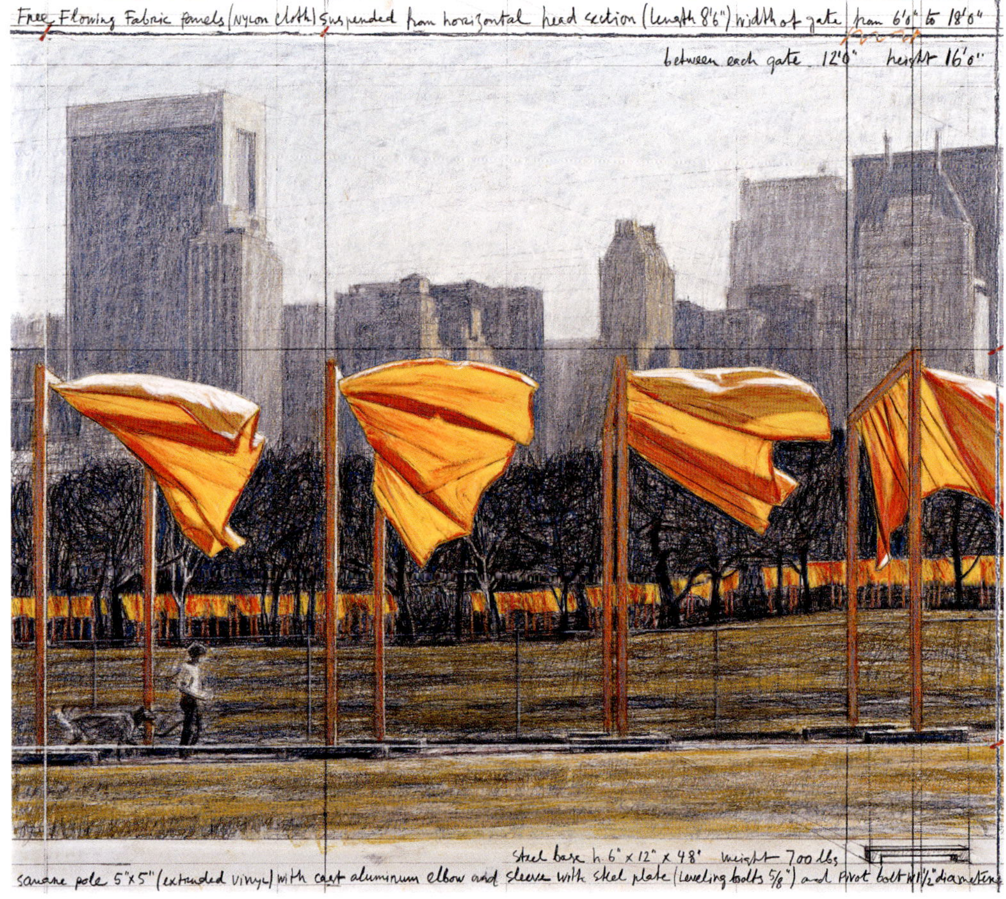

The Gates, Project for Central Park, New York City
Collage in two parts, 2003
12 x 30 ½ in., 26 ¼ x 30 ½ in.
Photo: Wolfgang Volz

THE GATES, PROJECT FOR CENTRAL PARK NEW YORK CITY

On January 22, 2003, Michael R. Bloomberg, Mayor of New York City, announced that the city has given permission to New York artists Christo and Jeanne-Claude to realize their temporary work of art: *The Gates, Central Park, New York City*, 1979–2005.

The 7500 Gates, 16 ft high with a width varying from 6 to 18 ft will follow the edges of the walkways and will be perpendicular to the selected 23 miles of footpaths in Central Park. Free hanging saffron colored fabric panels suspended from the horizontal top part of the gates will come down to approximately 7 ft above the ground. The gates will be spaced at 10 to 15 ft intervals allowing the synthetic woven panels to wave horizontally towards the next gate and be seen from far away through the leafless branches of the trees. The temporary work of art *The Gates* is scheduled for February 2005, to remain for 16 days, then the 7,500 Gates shall be removed and the materials will be recycled.

As Christo and Jeanne-Claude have always done for their previous projects, *The Gates* will be entirely financed by the artists through C.V.J. Corp, (Jeanne-Claude Javacheff, President) with the sale of studies, preparatory drawings and collages, scale models, earlier works of the Fifties and Sixties, and original lithographs on other subjects.

The artists do not accept sponsorship of any kind.

Neither New York City nor the Park administration shall bear any of the expenses for *The Gates*.

The Gates will provide employment for thousands of New York City residents:

- Manufacturing and assembling of the gates structures.
- Installation workers.
- Maintenance teams around the clock, in uniform and with radios.
- Removal workers.

The 5 in. sq vertical and horizontal poles will be extruded in 65 miles (104.6 km) of recyclable saffron colored vinyl. The vertical poles will be secured by 15,000 narrow, steel base footings, 600 lb each, positioned on the paved surfaces. There will be no holes in the ground.

The off-site fabrication of the gates structures and assembly of the 7,500 fabric panels made of 1,089,882 sq ft of fabric will be done in local workshops, and factories. The on-site installation of the bases, by small teams, spread in the park, will neither disturb the maintenance and management of Central Park nor the every day use of the park by the people of New York. The final installation of the 7,500 gates will be done simulatneously in five days by hundreds of workers.

The unfurling of the fabric panels will bloom in one day.

A written contract has been drafted between the City of New York and the Department of Parks and Recreation and the artists.

The contract requires the artists to provide, among other terms and conditions:

- Personal and property liability insurance holding harmless the City, the Department of Parks and Recreation and the Central Park Conservancy.
- Restoration Bond providing funds for complete removal.
- Full cooperation with the Department of Parks and Recreation, the Central Park Conservancy,

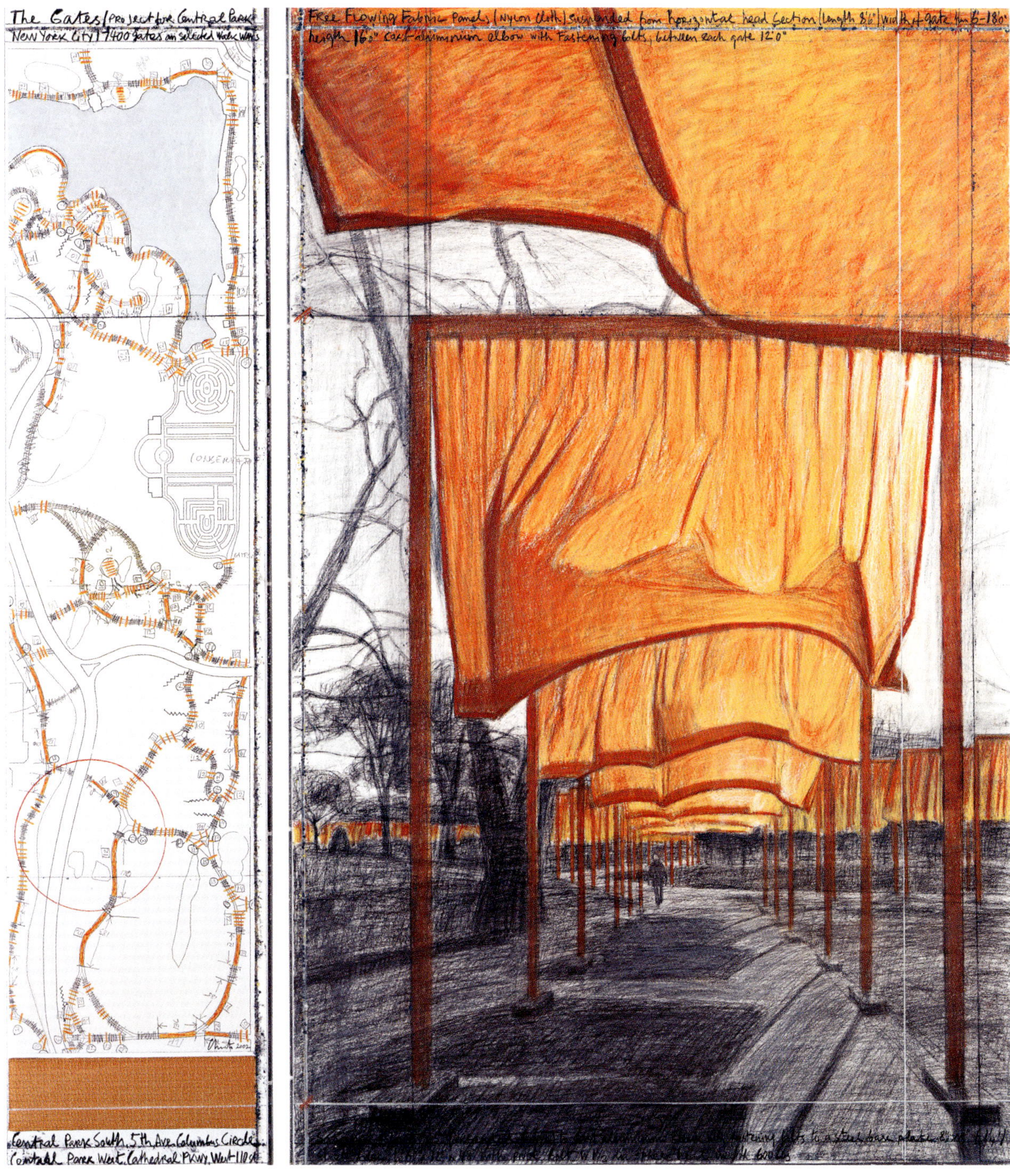

The Gates, Project for Central Park, New York City
Drawing in two parts, 2002
65 × 15 in., 65 × 42 in.

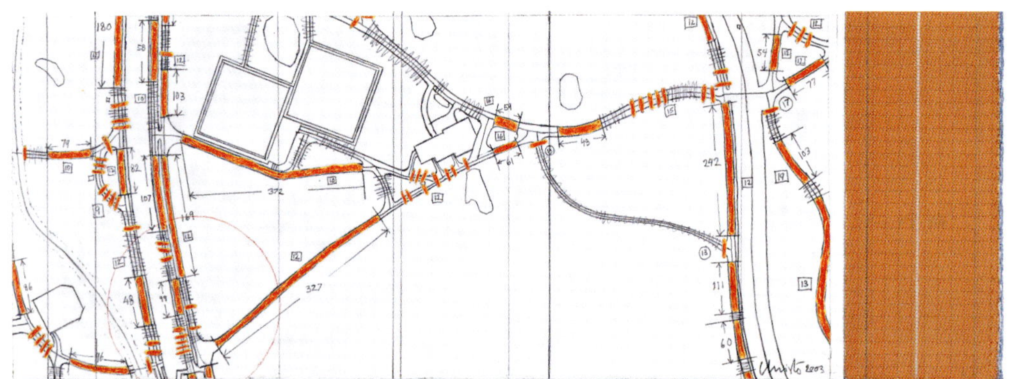

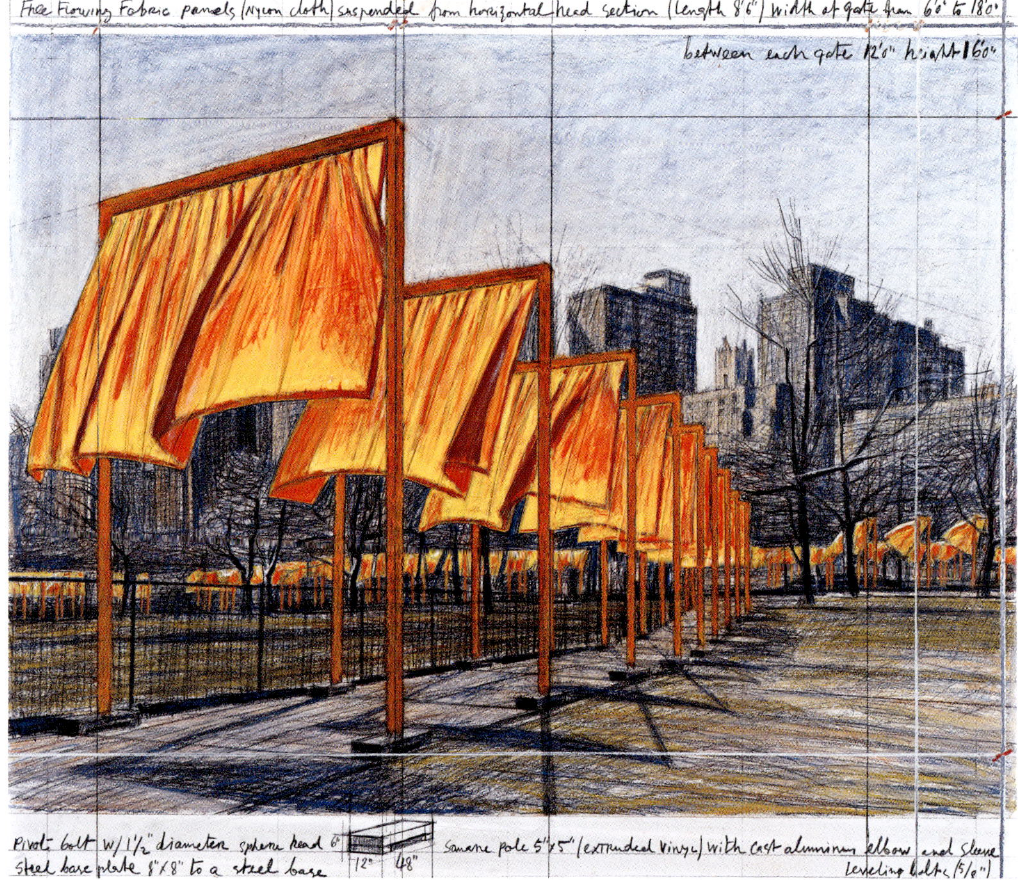

The Gates, Project for Central Park, New York City
Collage in two parts, 2003
12 x 30 ½ in., 26 ¼ x 30 ½ in.
Photo: Wolfgang Volz

the New York Police Department, the New York City Arts Commission, the Landmarks Commission and the Community Boards.

- Clearance for the usual activities in the park and access of Rangers, maintenance, clean-up, police and emergency vehicle.
- The artists shall pay all costs of the Park's supervision directly related to the project.
- Neither vegetation nor rock formations shall be disturbed.
- *The Gates* will be clear of rocks, tree roots and low branches.
- Only vehicles of small size will be used and will be confined to existing walkways during installation and removal.
- The people of New York will continue to use Central Park as usual.
- After the removal, the site shall be inspected by the Department of Parks and Recreation which will be holding the security until satisfaction.

For those who will walk through *The Gates*, following the walkways, and staying away from the grass, *The Gates* will be a golden ceiling creating warm shadows. When seen from the buildings surrounding Central Park, *The Gates* will seem like a golden river appearing and disappearing through the bare branches of the trees and will highlight the shape of the footpaths.

The 16 day duration work of art, free to all, will be a long-to-be-remembered joyous experience for every New Yorker, as a democratic expression that Olmsted invoked when he conceived a "central" park. The luminous moving fabric will underline the organic design of the park, while the rectangular poles will be a reminder fo the geometric grid pattern of the city blocks around the park. *The Gates* will harmonize with the beauty of Central Park.

Vince Davenport is the chief engineer and director of construction. Jonita Davenport is the project director.

All materials are being shipped to the rented 25,000 square foot assembly plant in Queens, NY. Six manufacturing plants are preparing the materials, plus a sewing plant.

Some of the materials ordered for 7,500 GATES (as of September 7, 2003):
(Numbers might change slightly.)

All materials will be recycled.

- 5,290 US tons of steel, 10,580,000 lb for 15,000 specially designed steel footing weights, varying between 615 and 837 lb each, according to the width of the gate.
  The weights are resting on the hard surface of the walkways. There will be no holes in Central Park.
- 315,491 linear ft (60 miles) (96.5 km) of Vinyl tube, 5 in. x 5 in. sq extruded in saffron color, recyclable, specially designed, (for each gate: 2 vertical 16 ft long, and one horizontal (varying between 6 and 18 ft, because the width of the walkways varies)
- 15,000 specially designed, recyclable, cast aluminum upper corner reinforcements which hold together the 2 vertical poles to the horizontal pole.
- 15,000 base anchor sleeves. Which will be bolted to the steel footing weights.
  15,000 (½ in. x 8 in. x 8 in.) steel leveling plates. The leveling plate is between the base anchor sleeve and the steel base, it has a pivoting bolt which will ensure the perfect verticality of the poles, even when the walkways are inclined.
- 165,000 bolts and self-locking nuts. (7,500 x 8 ½ in.)
- 15,064 (8 x 8 x 8 in.) vinyl leveling plate covers, to hide the bolts.
- 116,389 miles (187,311 km) of nylon thread to be extruded in saffron color and specially woven into 1,092,200 sq ft of recyclable, rip-stop fabric, and then shipped to the sewing factory to be cut and sewn into 7,500 fabric panels of various widths. 46 miles (74 km) of hems.

On January 3, 2005, weather permitting, our professional workers will enter Central Park. Using forklifts and pallet jacks, they will place the 15,000 steel weights bases at their specific positions on the edges of the walkways, usually at 12 ft intervals, unless there are low branches.

On Monday, February 7, 2005, weather permitting, approximately 700 non-skilled workers (in teams of seven) will elevate The Gates assemblies – two vertical and one horizontal pole, the upper and lower aluminum corners and base assembly and the fabric panel in a cocoon, attached to the upper horizontal pole. The fabric panels will not initially be seen because they will be restrained in the cocoons which will remain closed until Saturday, February 12, when all the cocoons will be opened, in one day (maybe in one morning), weather permitting, as with all our projects.

The Gates will remain in Central Park for 16 days, then the removal will start.

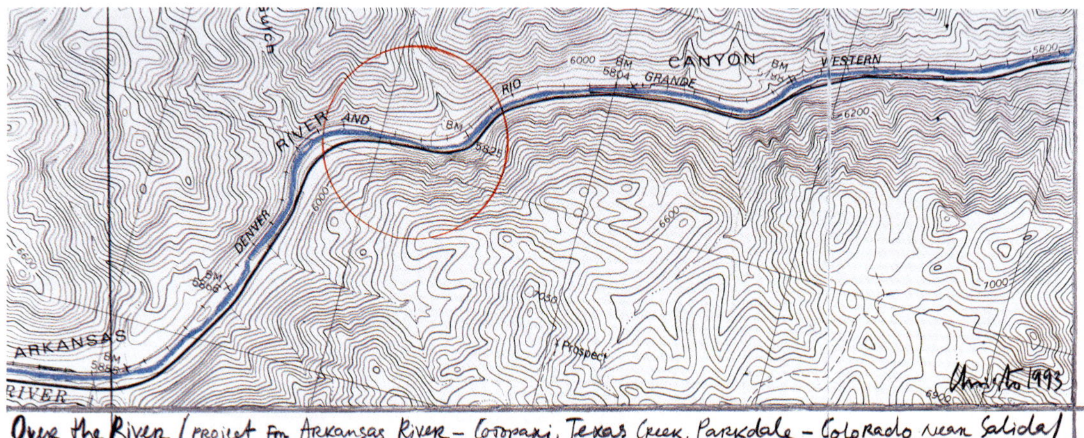

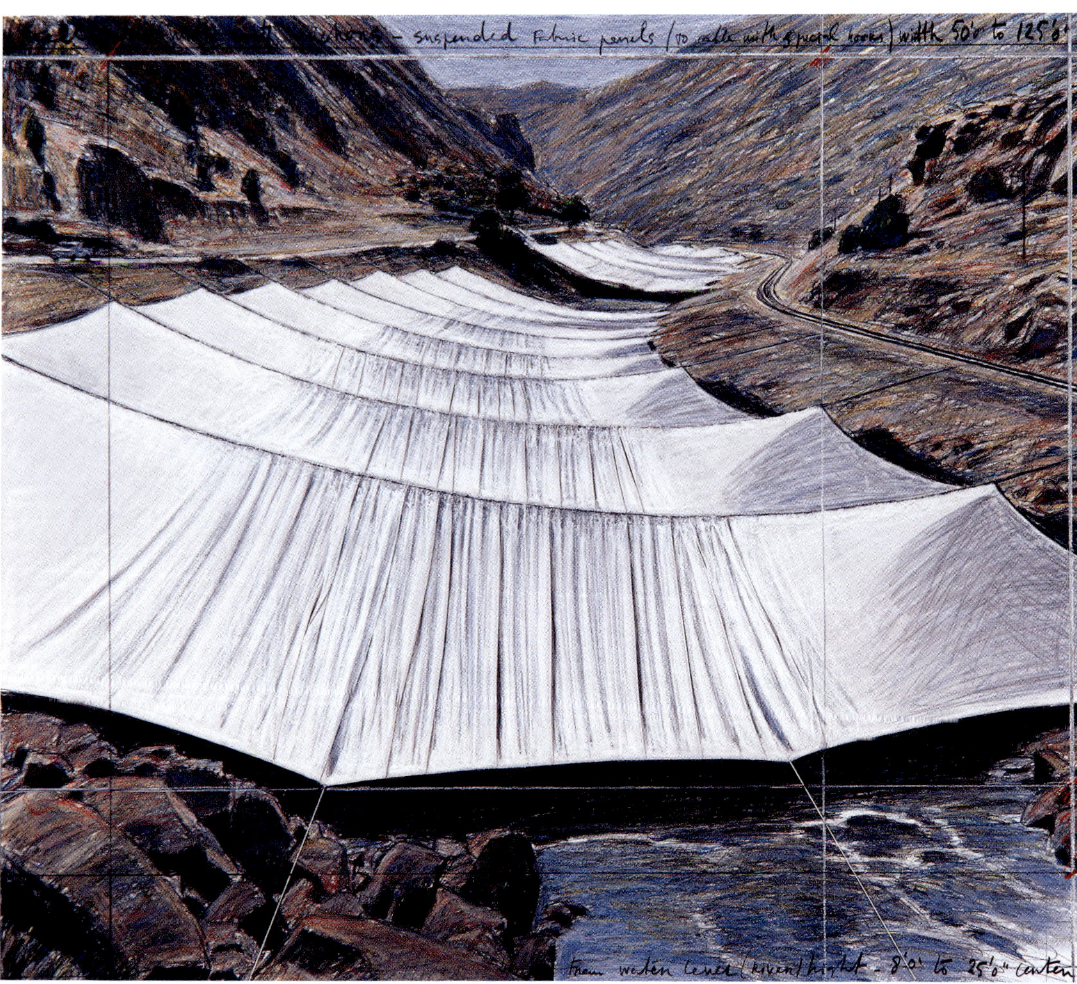

Over the River, Project for Arkansas River, Colorado
Collage (in two parts), 1993
12 x 30 ½ in., 26 ¼ x 30 ½ in.

OVER THE RIVER, Project for Arkansas River, Colorado, 1993

In progress

Fabric panels suspended horizontally clear of and high above the water level will follow the configuration and width of the changing course of the river, during a period of two consecutive weeks to be selected between mid-July and mid-August.

Steel wire cables, anchored on the upper part of the river banks, will cross the river and serve as attachment for the fabric panels.

The woven fabric panels, sewn in advance, with rows of grommets at the edges perpendicular to the river, will create shimmering waves of fabric, 10 to 23 ft above the river bed. The 6.7 mile (10.7 km) long stream of successive panels, will be interrupted by bridges, rocks, trees, bushes, and for esthetic reasons, creating abundant flows of light.

Wide clearance between the banks and the edges of the fabric panels will create a play of contrast allowing sunlight to illuminate the river on both sides. When seen from underneath, standing on the rocks at the edge of the river, at water level or by rafting, the luminous and translucent fabric will highlight the contours of the clouds, the mountains and the vegetation.

As with our previous art projects, *Over The River* will be entirely financed by Christo and Jeanne-Claude, through the sale by C.V.J. Corporation (Jeanne-Claude Christo-Javacheff, President) of Christo's preparatory drawings, lithographs, collages and early works. As it was done for past projects, most of the materials will be recycled.

In the USA, most of the rivers are born in the Rocky Mountains, some flowing east to the Mississippi River or the Gulf of Mexico, some flowing west to the Pacific Ocean. For the project, a river had to be chosen. That river should have high banks so that steel cables could be suspended, a road running continuously along the river, as well as both white and tranquil waters used for rafting.

During August 1992, 1993 and 1994, Christo and Jeanne-Claude traveled 14,000 miles (22,530 km) in the United States part of the Rocky Mountains in search of a site for the project with their collaborator-friends: Project director Tom Golden, Project Manager Richard Miller, Construction Manager, O. W. Vince Davenport, Jonita Davenport, Simon Chaput, Anna-Maryke Havekes, Wolfgang and Sylvia Volz, Masa Yanagi, Harrison Rivera-Terreaux, Vladimir Yavachev and John Kaldor.

During those trips the team prospected 89 rivers in the Rocky Mountains, in seven states, and six possible locations were found. After visiting the six sites again during the summer of 1996 the Arkansas River in Colorado was selected.

Vince Davenport and Wolfgang Volz organized life-size prototype tests for Christo and Jeanne-Claude and their technical team during June and September 1997, June 1998 and June 1999.
Tests have been conducted by Scott L. Gamble and Mark A. Hunter of R.W.D.I. Inc. Consulting Engineers in the wind tunnel in Guelph, Canada and at the site of the life-size test in Colorado, for the project's engineers Vince Davenport and John Thomson.

C. V. J. Corporation has retained the services of: Loren R. Hettinger and Teresa O'Neil of J. F. Sato and Associates, Consulting Engineers, Littleton, Colorado, to prepare the Environmental Assessment; Francis E. Harrison and Mark Juneau of Golder Associates Inc., Lakewood, Colorado to prepare the design engineering; Bryan Law and Richard Mariotti, of Law and Mariotti Consultants Inc., Colorado Springs, to prepare the topographic maps; David Ness and Donald Cleveland, M. J. Harden Inc., Kansas City, to prepare the aerial photography maps.

The road running along the river, and the existing footpaths leading to the water will allow the project to be seen, approached and enjoyed from above by car or bus, and from underneath on foot or by raft or kayak. For a period of two weeks, the temporary work of art Over The River will join the other recreational activities and the natural life of the river.

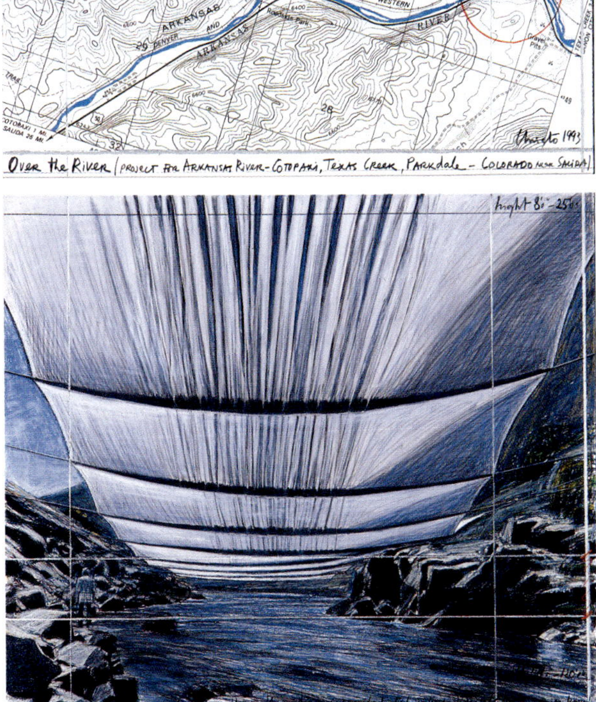

Over the River, Project for Arkansas River, Colorado
Collage (in two parts), 1993
12 x 30 ½ in., 26 ¼ x 30 ½ in.

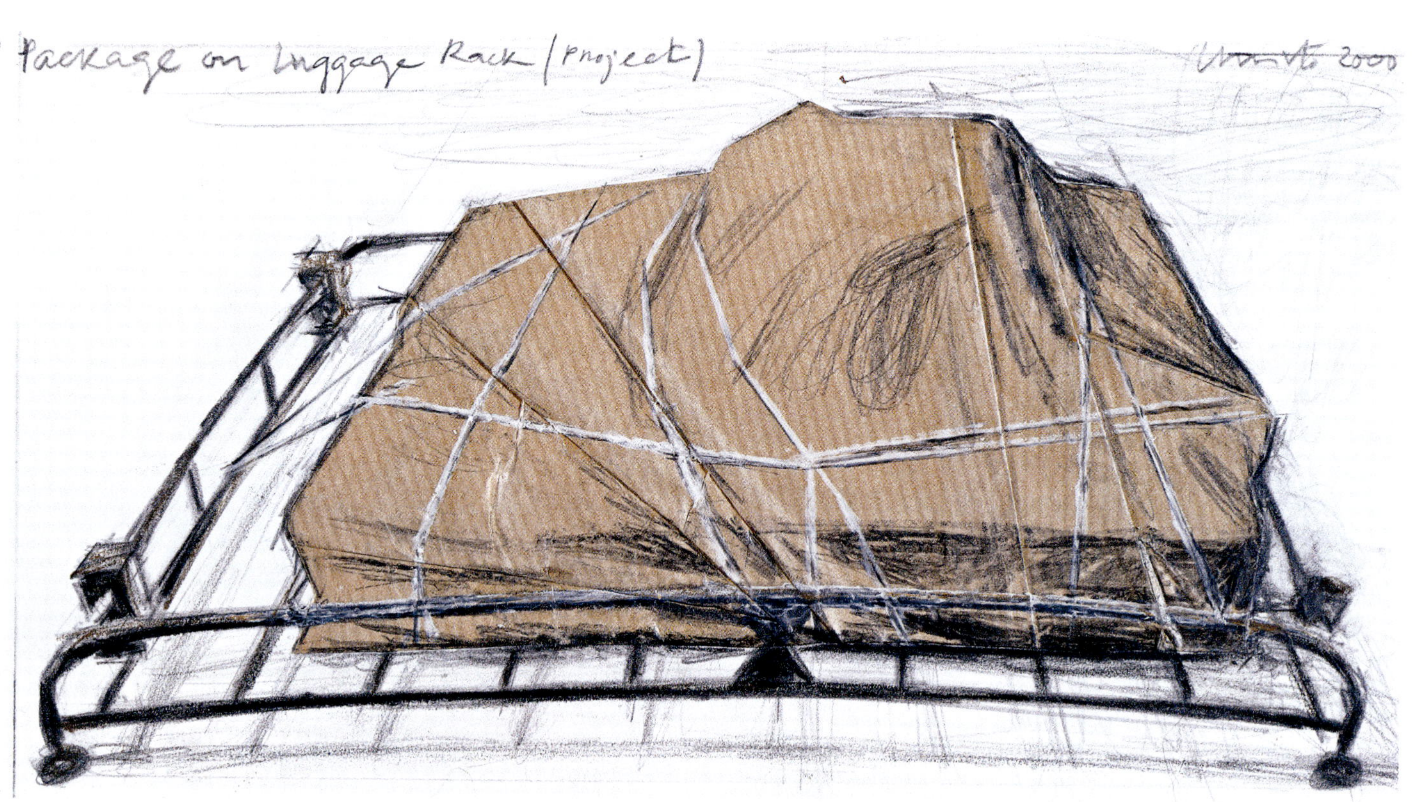

Package on Luggage Rack (Project)
Collage, 2000
4 ¾ x 8 ⅞ in.

Other Projects

Wrapped Oil Barrels, 1958/59
Wrapped Road Sign, 1963
Wrapped Road Sign (Project), 2000
Show Window, 1965/66
Wrapped Whitney Museum of American Art, Project for NY, 1967
Wrapped Opera House, Project for Sidney 1969–1990
The Mastaba of Abu Dhabi: Project for the United Arab Emirates, 1979
Ericsson Display Monitor Unit 3111. Wrapped Project for Personal Computer, 1985
Package on a Hunt, Project for Goslar, 1988
Package on a Hunt (Project for Goslar), 2000
Wrapped Floors and Stairways and Covered Windows, Project for the Würth Museum, 1994
Wrapped Floors and Stairways and Covered Windows, Project for the Würth Museum, 1994
Wrapped Floors and Stairways and Covered Windows, Project for the Würth Museum, 1994
Wrapped Floors and Stairways and Covered Windows, Project for the Würth Museum, Germany, 1994
Wrapped Tree, Project for the Museum Würth, Germany, 1994
Wrapped Violin, 1994
Wrapped Chairs, Wrapped Table, Wrapped Bar Table, and Wrapped Armchair, 1995
Otterlo Mastba (Project for Rijksmuseum Kroller-Muller, Holland), 2000
Package on a Table (Project), 2000
Package on Handtruck (Project), 2000
Package on Luggage Rack (Project), 2000
Package on Luggage Rack (Project), 2000
Package on Radio Flyer Wagon (Project), 2000
Pink Package on Baby Carriage (Project), 2000
Wool Bales Wrapped (Project for National Gallery of Victoria, Melbourne, Australia), 2000
Wrapped Armchair (Project), 2000
Wrapped Automobile (Project for Volvo 122-S Sport Sedan), 2000
Wrapped Baby Carriage (Project), 2000
Wrapped Carozza (Project), 2000

Wrapped Chair (Project), 2000
Wrapped Hay (Project), 2000
Wrapped magazines (For Reinhold Wurth), 2000
Wrapped Motorcycle (Project), 2000
Wrapped Statue/Sleeping Fawn (Project for the Glyptotheck, München), 2000
Wrapped Table and Chair (Project), 2000
Wrapped Telephone (Project), 2000
Wrapped Toy Horse (Project for Neo-Dada wrapped), 2000
Wrapped Tree (Project), 2000

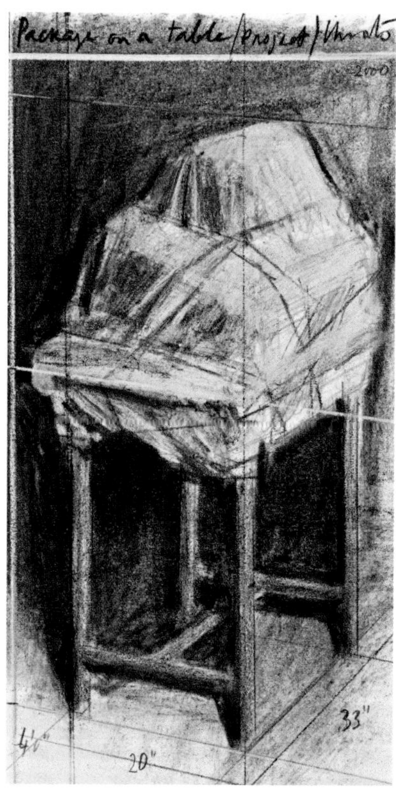

Package on a Table (Project)
Drawing, 2000
8 ⅞ x 4 ¾ in.

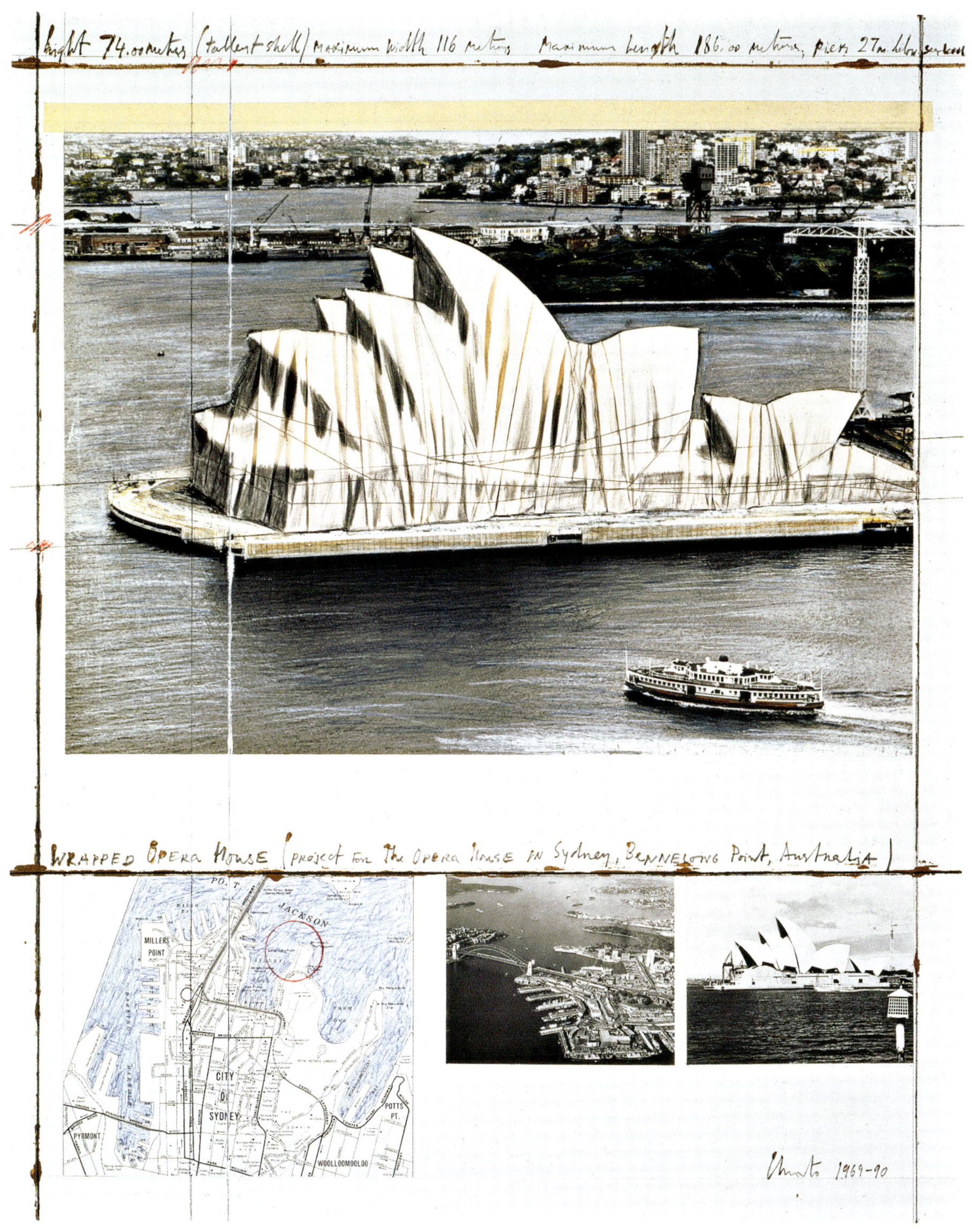

Wrapped Opera House, Project for Sidney
Hand collage lithograph, 1969–1990
30 ¼ x 24 ¾ in.

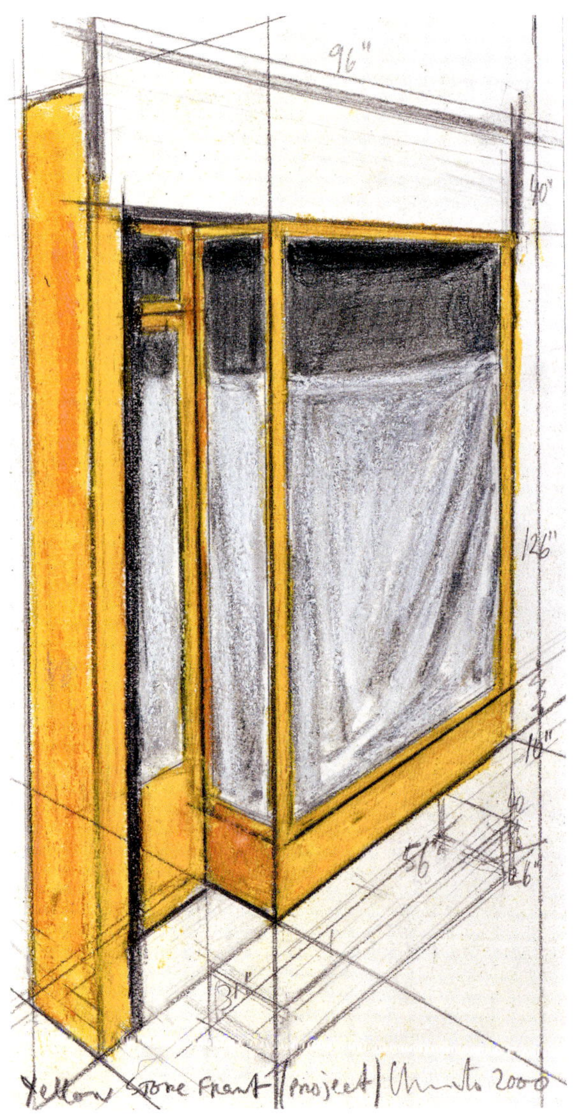

Yellow Store Front (Project)
Drawing, 2000
8 ⅞ x 4 ¾ in.

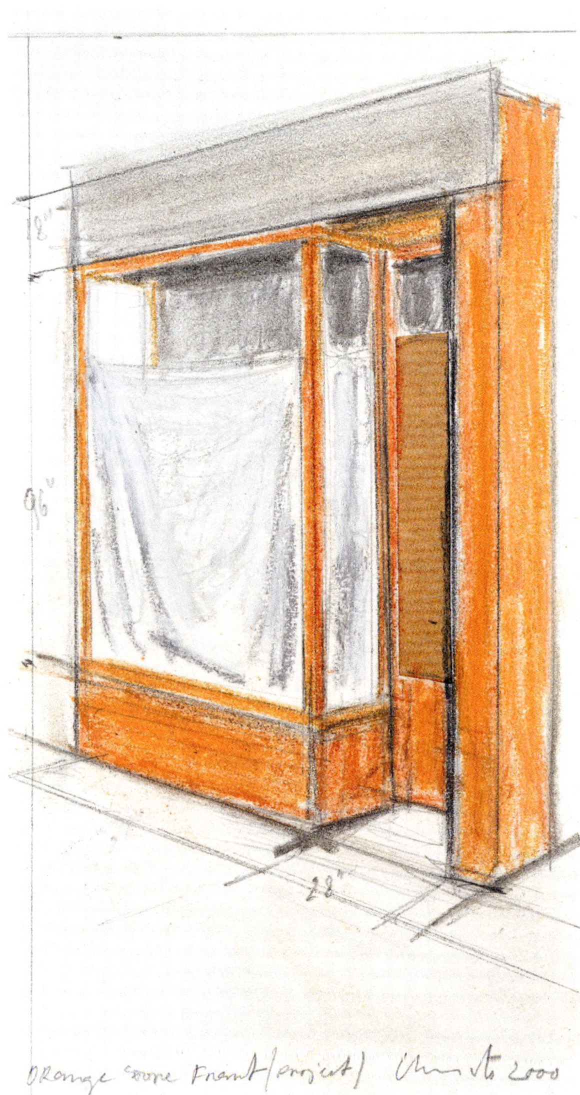

Orange Store Front (Project)
Collage, 2000
8 ⅞ x 4 ¾ in.

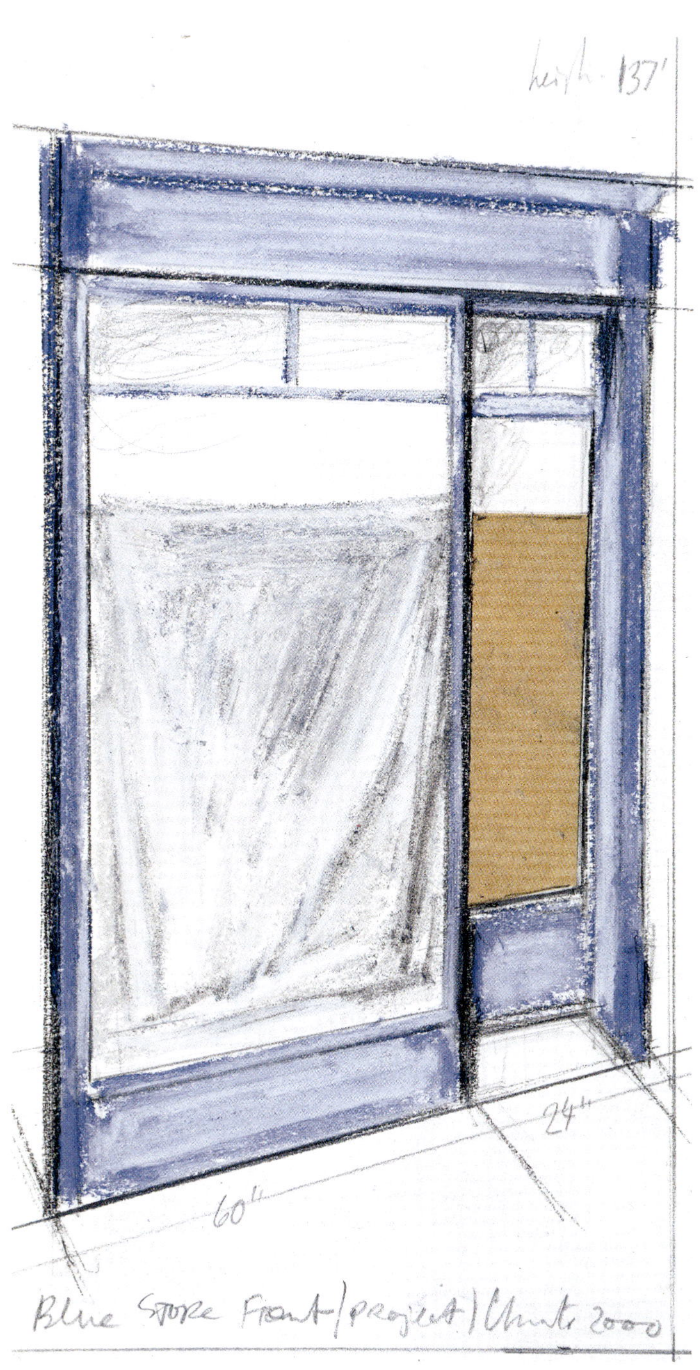

Blue Store Front (Project)
Collage, 2000
8 ⅞ x 4 ¾ in.

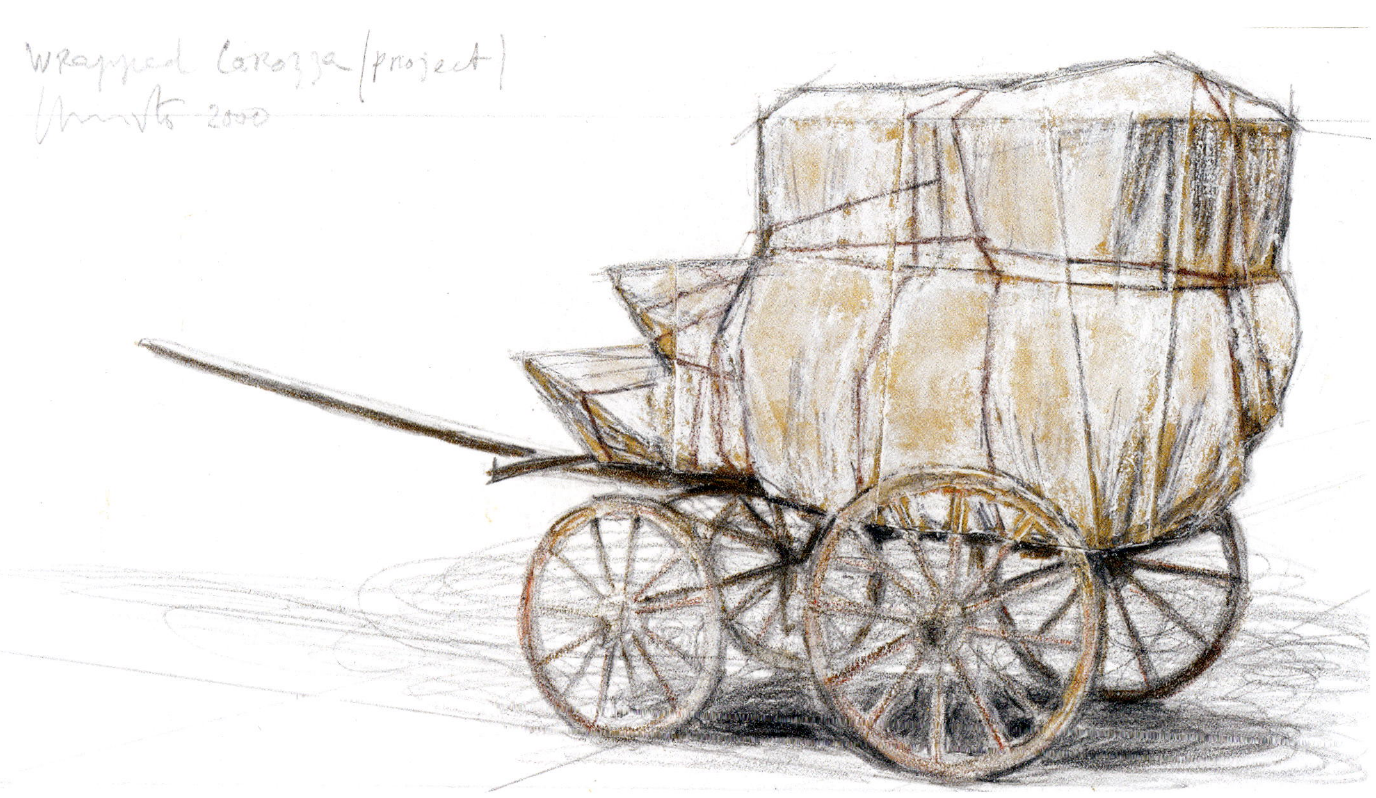

Wrapped Carozza (Project)
Collage, 2000
4 ¾ x 8 ⅞ in.

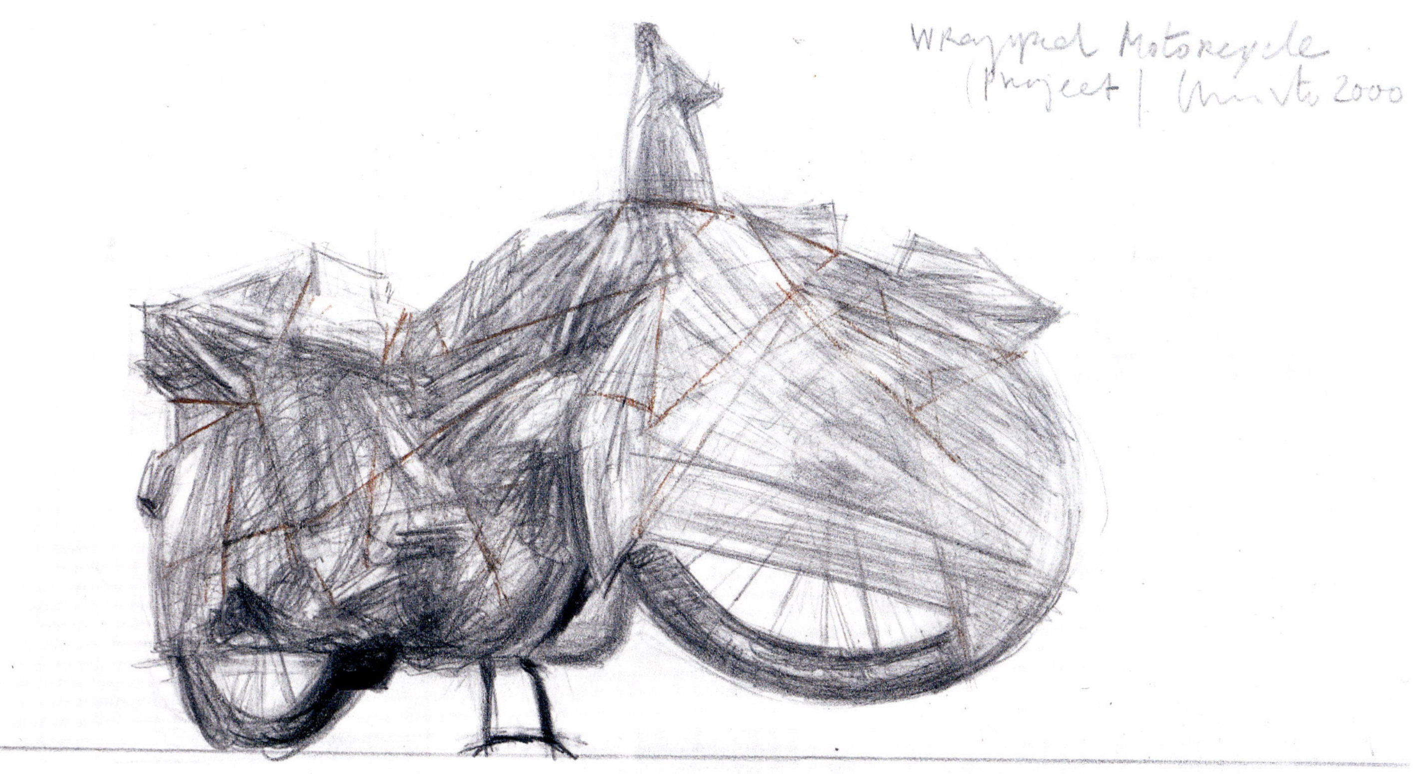

Wrapped Motorcycle (Project)
Drawing, 2000
4 ¾ x 8 ⅞ in.

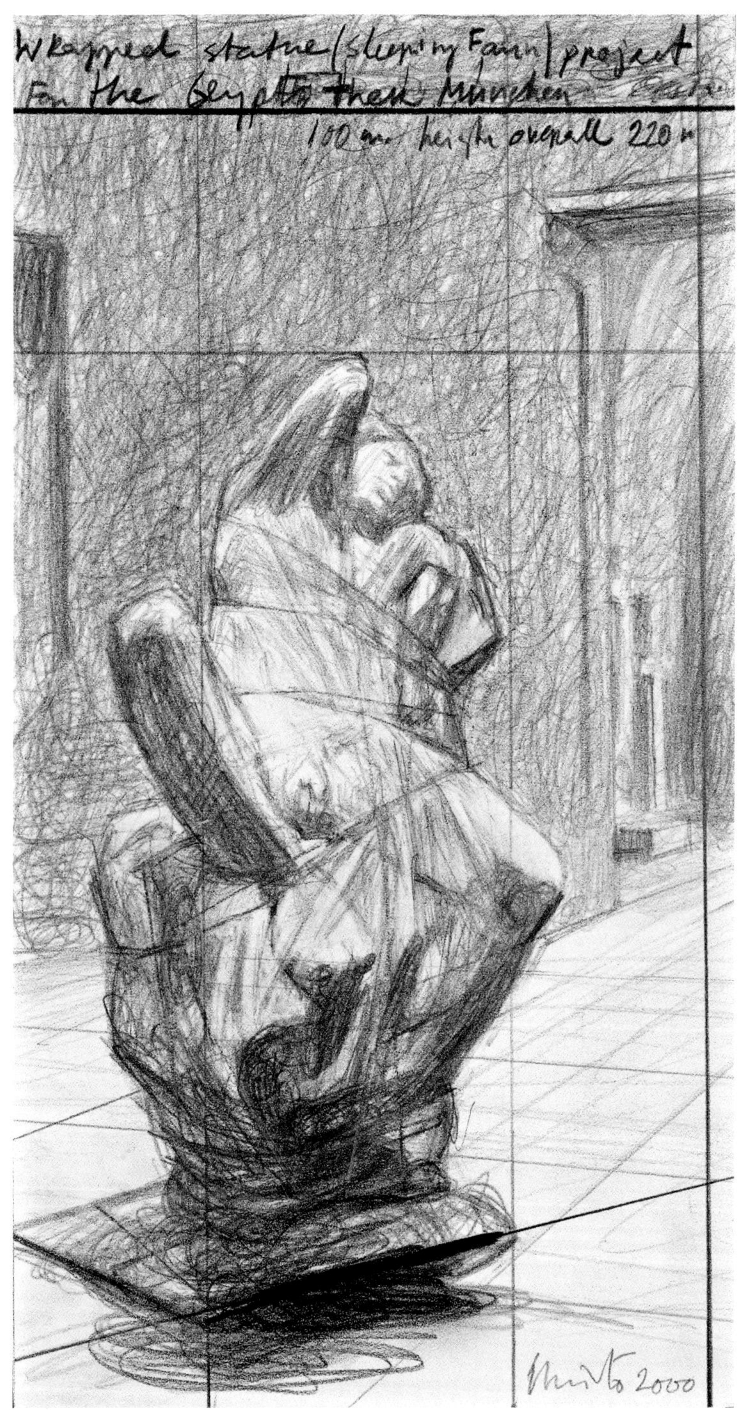

Wrapped Statue/Sleeping Fawn (Project for the Glyptotheck, München)
Drawing, 2000
8 ⅞ x 4 ¾ in.

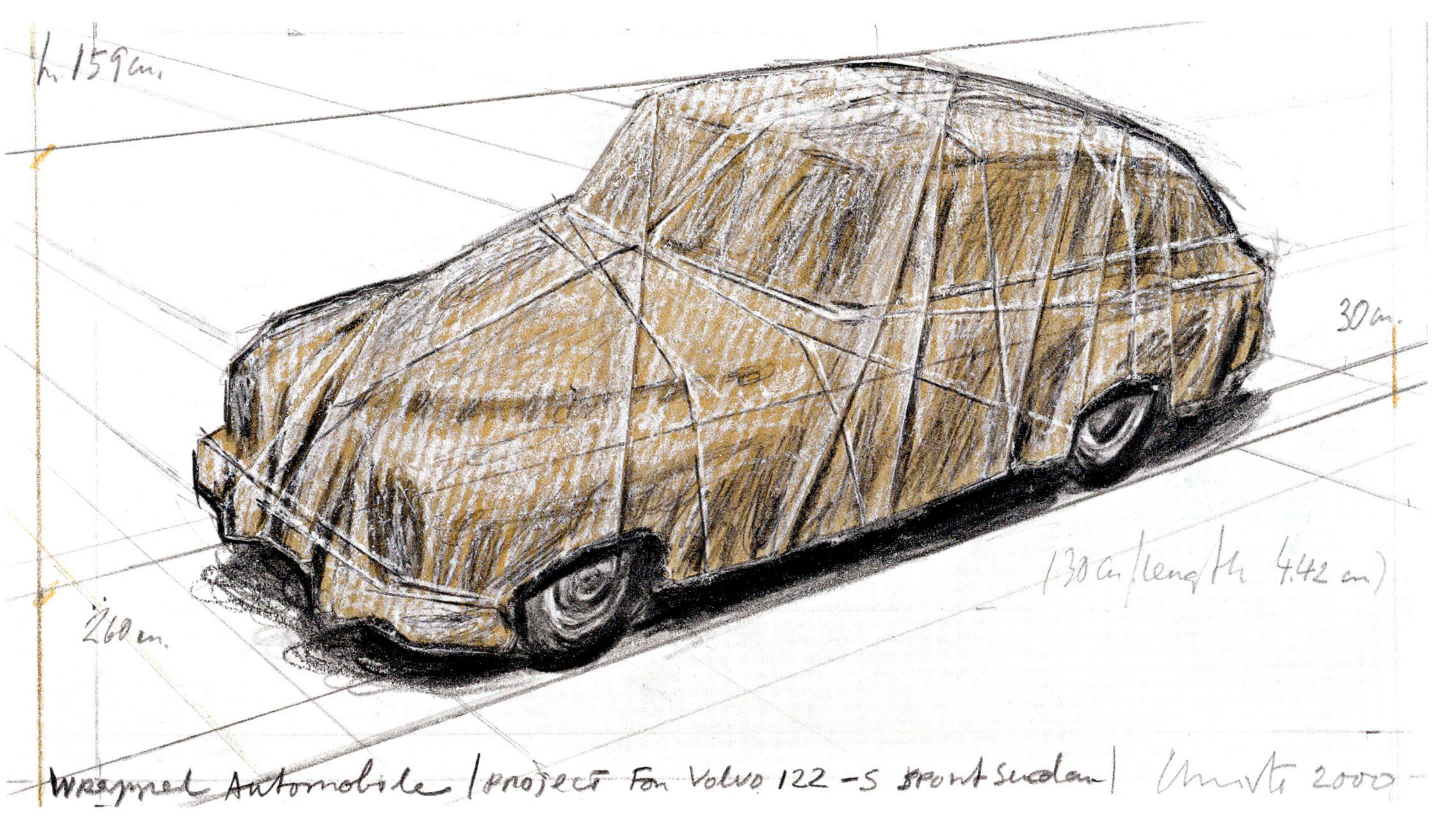

Wrapped Automobile (Project for Volvo 122-S Sport Sedan)
Collage, 2000
4 ¾ x 8 ⅞ in.

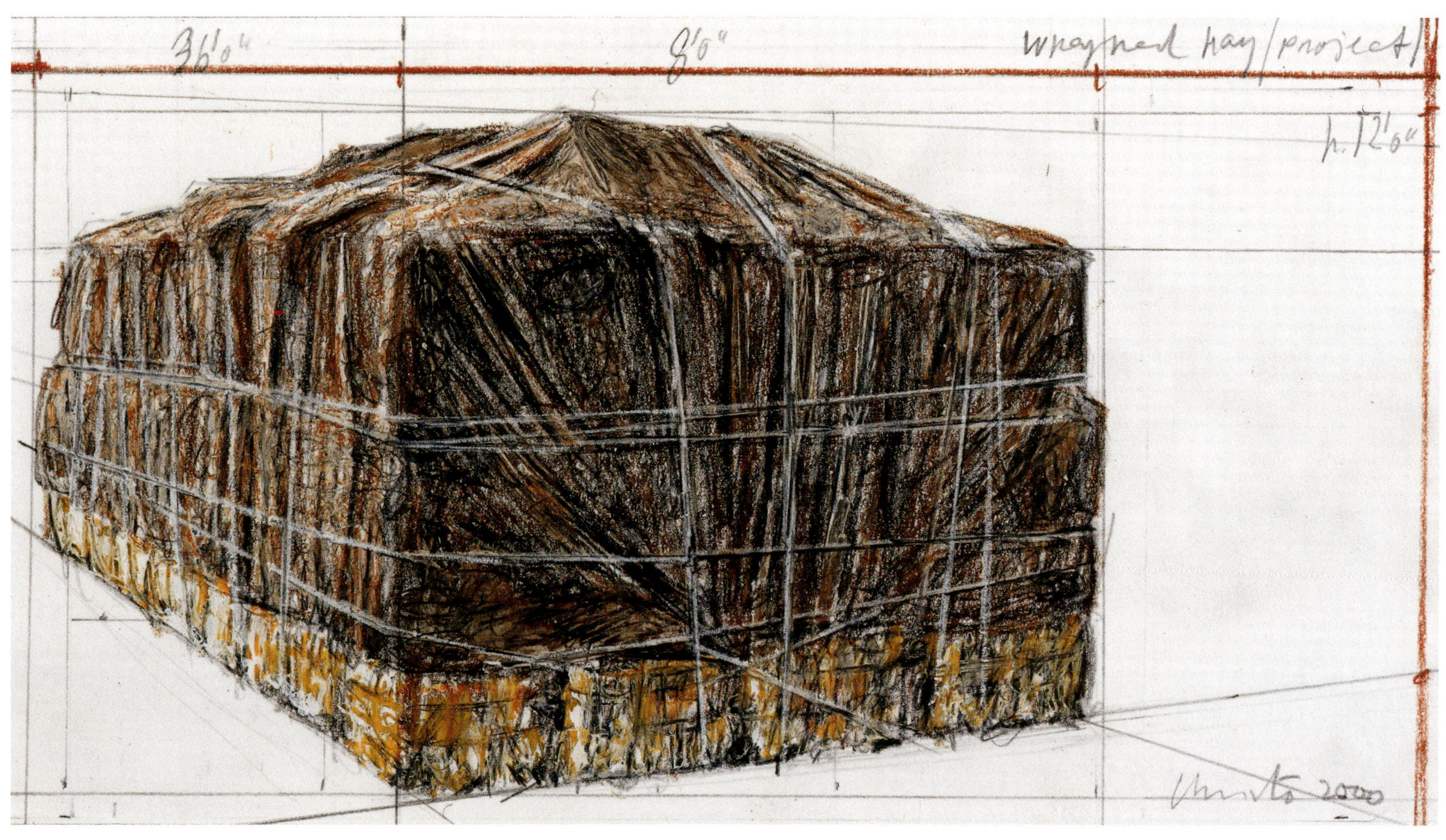

Wrapped Hay (Project)
Drawing, 2000
4 ¾ x 8 ⅞ in.

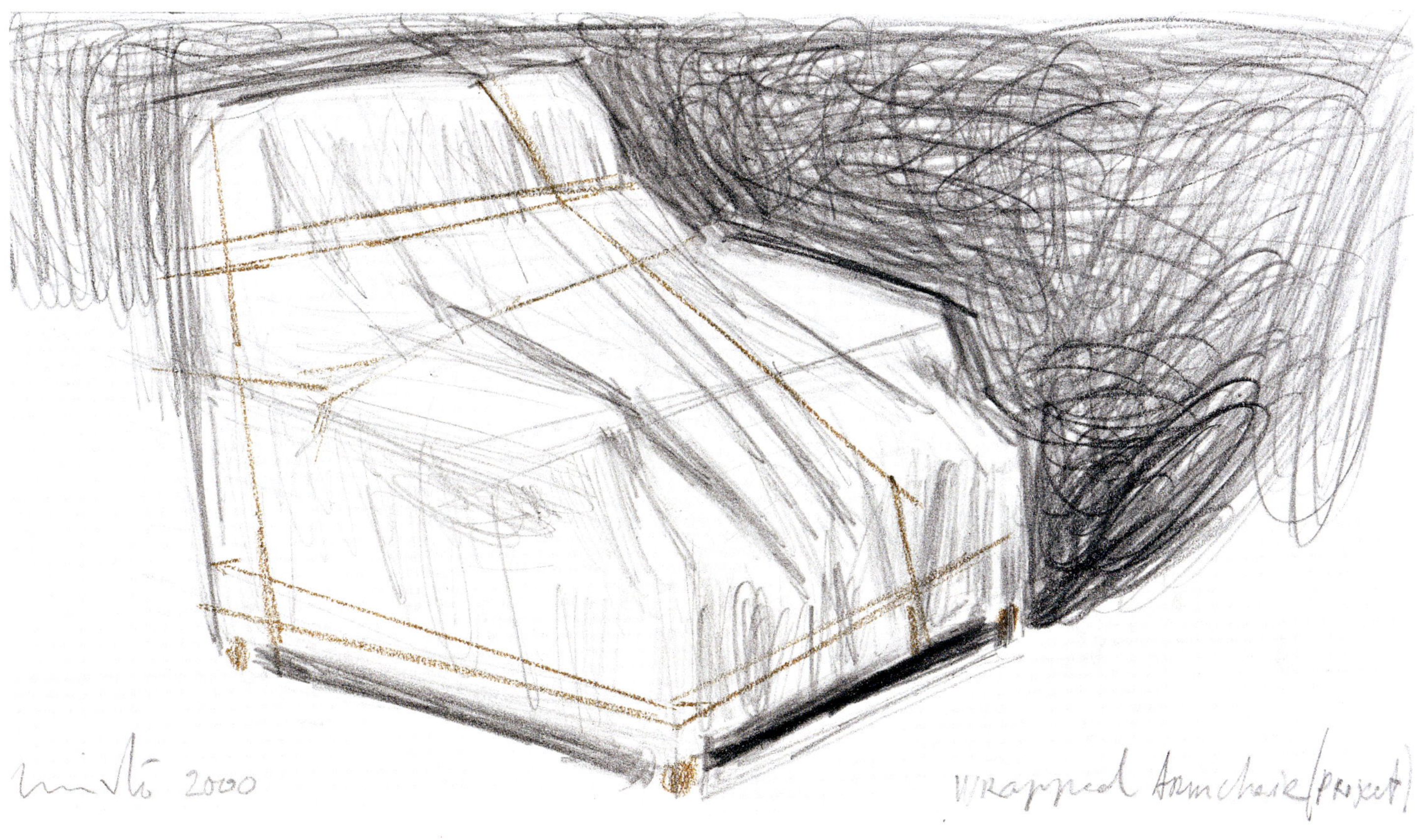

Wrapped Armchair (Project)
Drawing, 2000
4 ¾ x 8 ⅞ in.

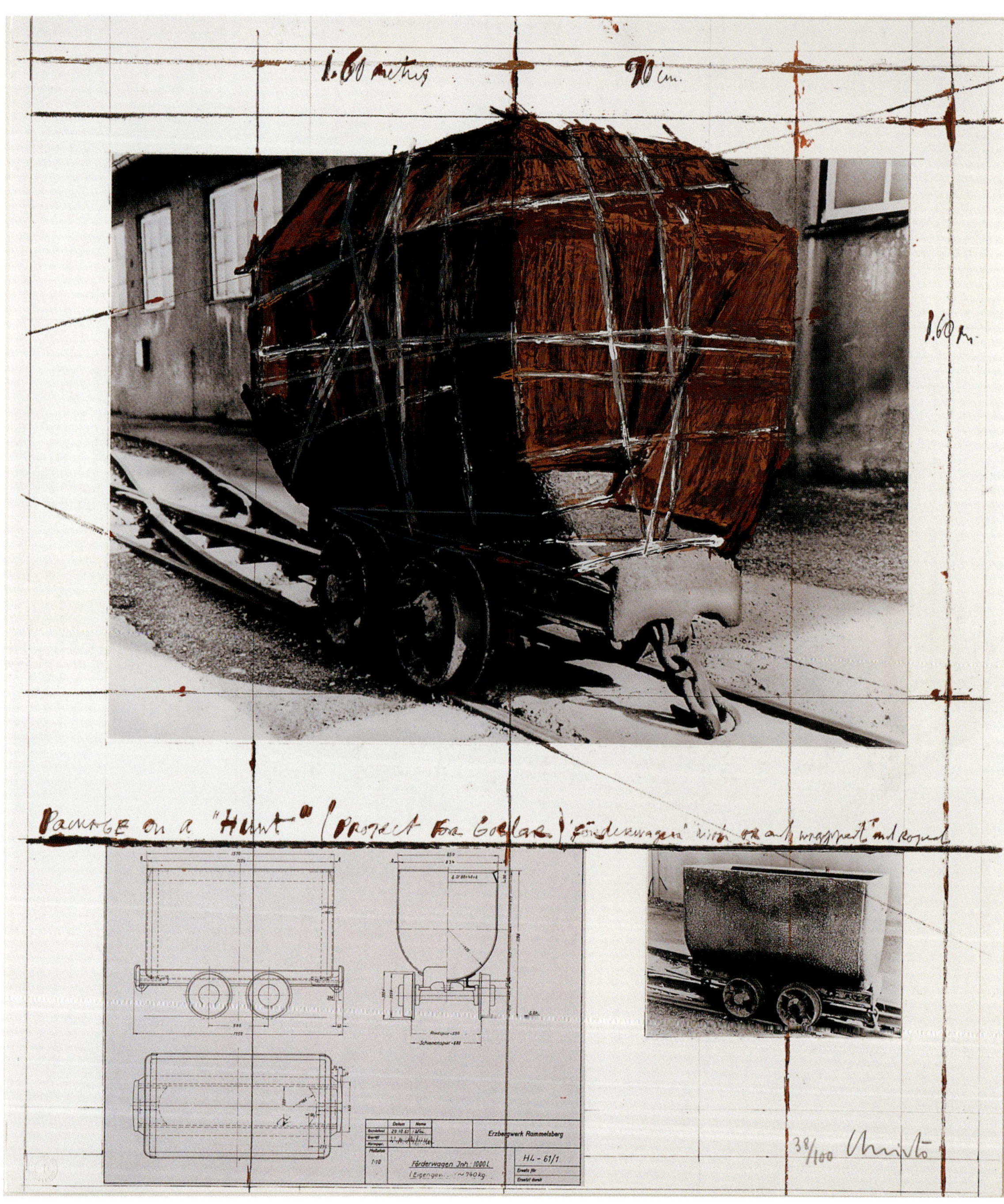

Package on a Hunt, Project for Goslar
Lithograph, 1988
27 ⅝ x 31 ½ in.

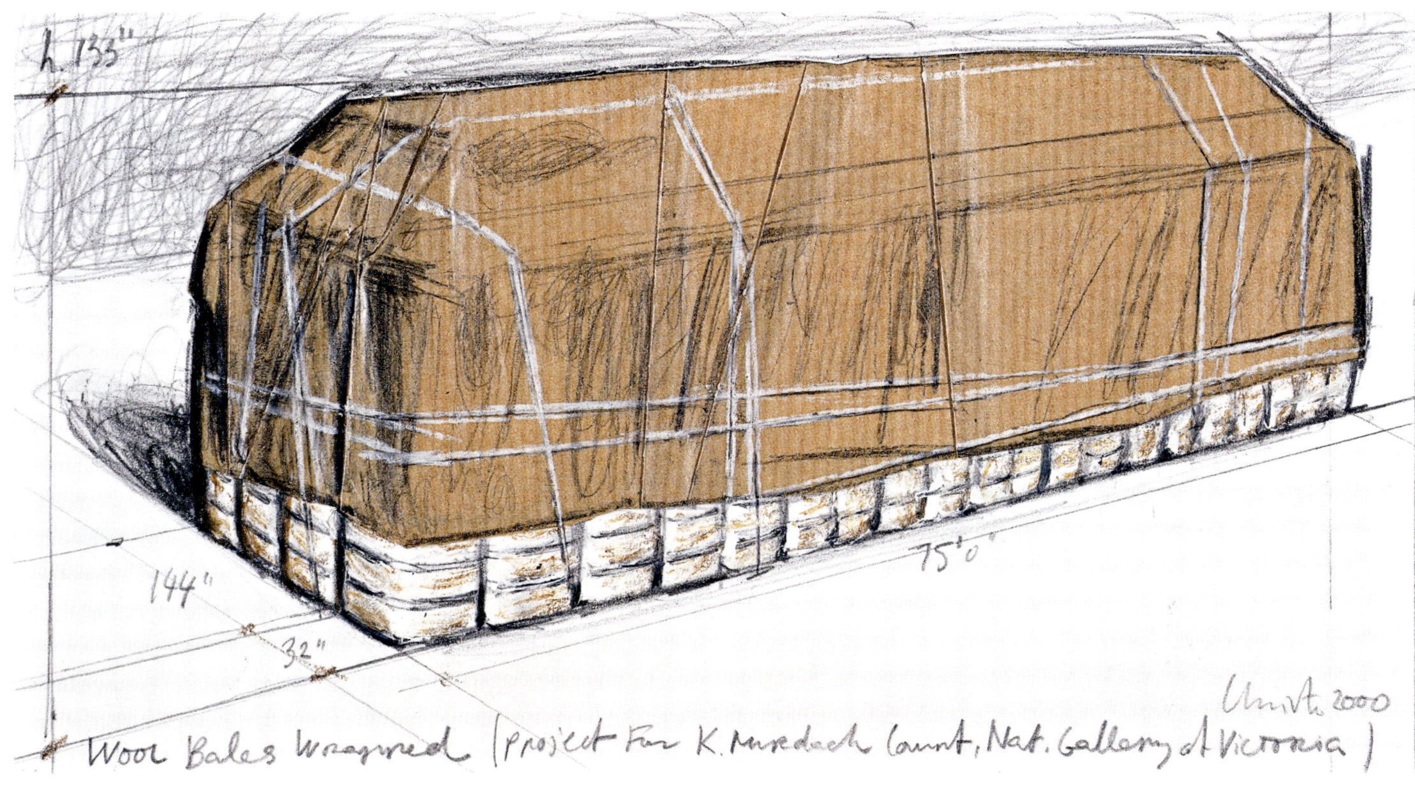

Wool Bales Wrapped (Project for National Gallery of Victoria, Melbourne, Australia)
Collage, 2000
4 ¾ x 8 ⅞ in.

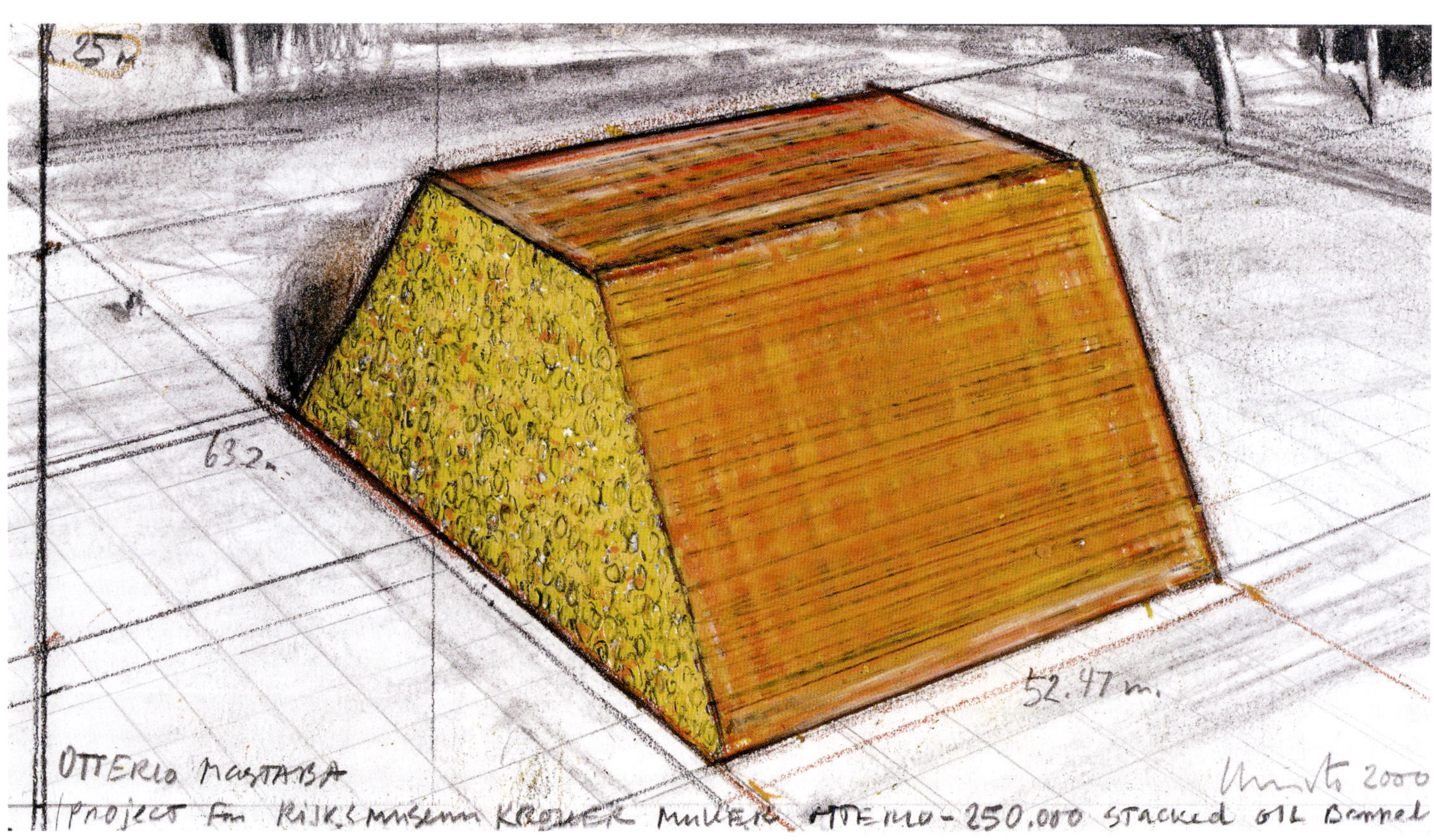

Otterlo Mastaba (Project for Rijksmuseum Kroller-Muller, Holland)
Drawing, 2000
4 ¾ x 8 ⅞ in.

BIBLIOGRAPHY

Selected further reading from the Christo and Jeanne-Claude website:

BOOKS:

1965 *Christo.* Texts by David Bourdon, Otto Hahn and Pierre Restany. Designed by Christo. Edizioni Apollinaire, Milano, Italy.

1968 *Christo: 5,600 Cubic Meter Package.* Photographs by Klaus Baum. Designed by Christo. Verlag Wort und Bild, Baierbrunn, Germany.

1969 *Christo.* Text by Lawrence Alloway. Designed by Christo. Harry N. Abrams Publications, New York, USA. Verlag Gerd Hatje, Stuttgart, Germany. Thames and Hudson, London, England.

1969 *Christo: Wrapped Coast, One Million Square Feet.* Photographs by Shunk-Kender. Designed by Christo. Contemporary Art Lithographers, Minneapolis, USA.

1970 *Christo.* Text by David Bourdon. Designed by Christo. Harry N. Abrams Publications, New York, USA.

1971 *Christo: Projeckt Monschau.* By Willi Bongard. Verlag Art Actuell, Köln, Germany.

1973 *Christo: Valley Curtain.* Photographs by Harry Shunk. Designed by Christo. Verlag Gert Hatje, Stuttgart, Germany; Harry N. Abrams Publications, New York, USA. Pierre Horay, Paris, France. Gianpaolo Prearo, Milano, Italy.

1975 *Christo: Ocean Front.* Text by Sally Yard and Sam Hunter. Photographs by Gianfranco Gorgoni. Edited by Christo. Princeton University Press, New Jersey, USA.

1975 *Environmental Impact Report: Running Fence.* Prepared by Paul E. Zigman and Richard Cole, Environmental Science Associates Inc. Foster City, California, USA.

1977 *Christo: The Running Fence.* Text by Werner Spies. Photographs and editing by Wolfgang Volz. Harry N. Abrams, Inc., New York, USA. (in English). Édition du Chêne, Paris, France (in French). Editions Gerd Hatje, Stuttgart, Germany (in German).

1978 *Christo: Running Fence.* Chronicle by Calvin Tomkins. Narrative text by David Bourdon. Photographs by Gianfranco Gorgoni. Designed by Christo. Harry N. Abrams, Inc., New York, USA.

1978 *Christo: Wrapped Walk Ways.* Essay by Ellen Goheen. Photographs by Wolfgang Volz. Designed by Christo. Harry N. Abrams, Inc., New York, USA.

1980 *Catalogue Raisonné of original works.* Being prepared by Daniel Varenne. with the collaboration of Ariane Coppier, Marie-Claude Blancpain and Raphaëlle de Pourtales, in progress.

1982 *Christo-Complete Editions 1964-82.* Catalogue Raisonné. Introduction by Per Hovdenakk. Verlag Schellmann and Kluser, München, Germany. New York University Press, New York, USA.

1984 *Christo: Works 1958-83.* Text by Yusuke Nakahara. Publication Sogetsu Shuppan, Inc., Tokyo, Japan.

1984 *Christo: Surrounded Islands, Biscayne Bay, Greater Miami, Florida, 1980-83* Text by Werner Spies, photographs and editing by Wolfgang Volz. Dumont Buchverlag, Köln, Germany. Harry N. Abrams, Inc., New York, USA, 1985. Fondation Maeght, Saint-Paul de Vence, France, 1985. Ediciones Poligrafa, Barcelona, Spain, 1986.

1984 *Christo-Der Reichstag.* Compiled by Michael Cullen and Wolfgang Volz. Photographs by Wolfgang Volz. Suhrkamp Verlag, Frankfurt, Germany.

1985 *Christo.* Text by Dominique Laporte. Publication: Art Press /Flammarion, Paris, France. English edition by Pantheon Books, New York, USA, 1986.

1986 *Christo: Surrounded Islands, Biscayne Bay, Greater Miami, Florida, 1980-83.* Photographs by Wolfgang Volz. Introduction and Picture Commentary by David Bourdon. Essay by Jonathan Fineberg. Report by Janet Mulholland. Designed by Christo. Harry N. Abrams, Inc., New York, USA.

1987 *Le Pont-Neuf de Christo, Ouvrage d'Art, Oeuvre d'Art, ou Comment Se Faire une Opinion.* By Nathalie Heinich. Photographs by Wolfgang Volz. A.D.R.E.S.S.E. Publication

1987 *Helt Fel I Paris.* By Pelle Hunger and Joakim Stromholm. Photographs by J. Stromholm. Butler and Tanner Ltd. The Selwood Printing Works, Fromme, England.

1988 *Christo: Prints and Objects, 1963-1987.* Catalogue Raisonné edited by Jörg Schellmann and Josephine Benecke. Introduction by Werner Spies. Editions Schellmann, München, Germany. Abbeville Press, New York, USA.

1990 *Christo: The Pont Neuf Wrapped, Paris, 1975-85.* Photographs by Wolfgang Volz. Texts by David Bourdon and Bernard de Montgolfier. Designed by Christo. Harry N. Abrams Inc., New York, USA. Adam Biro, Paris, France. Dumont Buchverlag, Köln, Germany.

1990 *Christo.* By Yusuke Nakahara, Shinchosha Co., Ltd., Tokyo, Japan.

1990 *Christo.* By Marina Vaizey. Poligrafa, Barcelona, Spain. Rizzoli, New York, USA. Albin Michel, Paris, France. Meulenhoff/Landshoff, Amsterdam, Holland. Verlag Aurel Bongers, Recklinghausen, Germany. Bijutsu Shupan-Sha, Tokyo, Japan.

1991 *Christo: The Accordion-Fold Book for The Umbrellas, Joint Project for Japan and U.S.A.* Photographs by Wolfgang Volz. Foreword and interview by Masahiko Yanagi. Designed by Christo. Chronicle Books, San Francisco, USA.

1993 *Christo: The Reichstag and Urban Projects.* Edited by Jacob Baal-Teshuva. Photographs by Wolfgang Volz. Contributions by Tilmann Buddensieg, Michael S. Cullen, Rita Süssmuth and Masahiko Yanagi. In German for the exhibitions at the Kunsthaus Wien, Austria – the Villa Stûch, Munich – and the Ludwig Museum, Aachen. Prestel Publications, München, Germany. In English for Prestel Publications, USA.

1994 *Christo and Jeanne-Claude: Der Reichstag und Urbane Projekte.* Edited by Jacob Baal-Teshuva. Contributions by Tilmann Buddensieg and Wieland Schmied. Interview by Masahiko Yanagi. Chronology by Michael S, Cullen. Photographs by Wolfgang Volz. Prestel Verlag, München, Germany.

1995 *Christo & Jeanne-Claude.* By Jacob Baal-Teshuva. Photographs by Wolfgang Volz. Designed by Christo. Edited by Simone Philippi and Charles Brace. Benedikt Taschen Verlag GmbH, Köln, Germany.

1995 *Christo, Jeanne-Claude, Der Reichstag dem Deutschen Volke.* By Michael S. Cullen and Wolfgang Volz. Photographs by Wolfgang Volz. Bastei-Lübbe, Gustav Lübbe Verlag GmbH, Bergisch-Gladbach, Germany.

1995 *Christo and Jeanne-Claude, Prints and Objects 1963-95.* Catalogue Raisonné. Edited by Jörg Schellmann and Joséphine Benecke. Editions Schellmann, München-New York. Schirmer Mosel Verlag München, Germany.

1995 *Christo & Jeanne-Claude Postcard Book.* Benedikt Taschen Verlag GmbH, Köln, Germany.

1995 *Christo & Jeanne-Claude, Poster Book.* Photographs by Wolfgang Volz. Text by Thomas Berg, Bonn, Benedikt Taschen Verlag GmbH, Köln, Germany.

1995 *Christo and Jeanne-Claude: Wrapped Reichstag, Berlin, 1971-95.* The Project Book. Photographs by Wolfgang Volz. Benedikt Taschen Verlag, GmbH, Köln, Germany.

1996 *Christo and Jeanne-Claude, Wrapped/Verhüllter Reichstag, Berlin 1971-1995.* Photographs by Wolfgang Volz. Picture Notes by David Bourdon. Edited by Simone Philippi. Designed by Christo. 700 pages. Benedikt Taschen Verlag GmbH, Köln, Germany.

Christo and Jeanne-Claude Projects selected from the Lilja Collection. Second Edition. Photographs by Wolfgang Volz. Preface by Torsten Lilja. Text by Per Hovdenakk. Azimuth Editions Limited, London, England.

1998 *Christo and Jeanne-Claude, The Umbrellas, Japan-USA, 1984-91.* Photographs by Wolfgang Volz, Picture notes by Jeanne-Claude and Masa Yanagi. Designed by Christo. Edited by Simone Philippi. 1,400 pages, two volumes in one box. Benedikt Taschen Verlag GmBH, Köln, Germany.

1998 Christo and Jeanne-Claude, Wrapped Trees, 1997-98. Photographs and Picture Notes by Wolfgang and Sylvia Volz. Introduction by Ernst Beyeler. Edited by Simone Philippi. Benedikt Taschen Verlag GmBH, Köln, Germany. 136 pages.

1998 Erreurs les plus Fréquentes.. Edited by Jeanne-Claude. In French. Editions Jannink, Paris.
2000 Christo and Jeanne-Claude, Most Common Errors/Erreurs Les Plus Fréquentes. Edited by Jeanne-Claude English and French. Edition Jannink, Paris.

2000 XTO + J-C. Christo und Jeanne-Claude, Eine Biografie von Burt Chernow, Epilog von Wolfgang Volz. In German. 496 pages, 55 illustrations plus 28 in color. (in German) Verlag Kiepenheuer & Witsch, Köln, Germany

2001 XTO + J-C. Christo e Jeanne-Claude, Una Biografia di Burt Chernow, Epilogo di Wolfgang Volz. (in italian) 366 pages, 99 illustrations, plus 28 in color. Publication Fondazione Ambrosetti Arte Contemporanea / Skira, Italy.

2002 *XTO + J-C. Christo and Jeanne-Claude*, a Biografie by Burt Chernow, Epilogue by Wolfgang Volz. (In English). Saint Martin's Press, New York.

2003 *Christo and Jeanne-Claude, The Gates, Project for Central Park, New York City.* Photographs by Wolfgang Volz. Picture Commentary by Jeanne-Claude and Jonathan Henery. Published by Hugh Lauter Levin Associates, Inc.

2004 *Christo and Jeanne-Claude: On the Way to the Gates.* Essay and Interviews by Jonathan Fineberg. Photographs by Wolfgang Volz. Picture Commentary by Jeanne-Claude and Jonathan Henery. Edited by Patricia Fidler; Designed and produced by Ken Wong. Yale University Press, New Haven, CT. and The Metropolitan Museum, New York City.

CATALOGUES
for Personal Exhibitions (partial listing):

1961 Galerie Haro Lauhus, Köln, Germany. Text by Pierre Restany. Poem by Stephan Wewerka.

1962 Rue Visconti, Paris. "Le Docker et le Décor." Text by Pierre Restany.

1966 Stedelijk van AbbeMuseum, Eindhoven, The Netherlands. Text by Lawrence Alloway.

1968 Museum of Modern Art, New York, USA. "Christo Wraps the Museum." Text by William Rubin.

1968 I.C.A. University of Pennsylvania, Philadelphia, USA. Text by Stephen Prokopoff.

1969 National Gallery of Victoria, Melbourne, Australia. "Woolworks." Text by Jan van der Marck.

1970–1972 Documentation Exhibition. Text by Maurice Besset.

1971 Haus Lange Museum, Krefeld, Germany. "Wrapped Floors, Covered Windows and Wrapped Walk Ways." Text by Paul Wember.

1971 Museum of Fine Arts, Houston, Texas, USA. "Valley Curtain, Project for Rifle, Colorado, in progress." Documentation . Text by Jan van der Marck.

1973 Kunsthalle, Düsseldorf, Germany, "Valley Curtain," Documentation Exhibition Text by John Matheson. Photographs by Harry Shunk.

1974 Musée de Peinture et de Sculpture, Grenoble, France. "Valley Curtain".

1975 Galerie Ciento, Barcelona, Spain. Text by Alexandre Cirici.

1975 Museo de Bellas Artes, Caracas. Exposicion Documental Sobre El "Valley Curtain. "Photographs by Harry Shunk. Impresion Editorial Arte, Caracas, Venezuela.

1977 Minami Gallery, Tokyo, Japan. Text by Yusuke Nakahara.

1977 Landische Museum, Bonn, Germany. "Wrapped Reichstag, Project for Berlin." Texts by Wieland Schmied and Tilmann Buddensieg.

1977 Annely Juda Fine Art, London, England." Wrapped Reichstag, Project for Berlin." Photographs by Wolfgang Volz. Texts by Wieland Schmied and Tilmann Buddensieg.

1978 Galerie Art in Progress, München, Germany. Galerien Maximilianstrasse. Text by Albrecht Haenlein.

1978 Rijksmuseum Kröller-Müller, Otterlo, The Netherlands. "The Mastaba." Introduction by R.W.D. Oxenaar and text by Ellen Joosten.

1979 Wiener Secession. Wien, Austria. "Running Fence," Documentation Exhibition. Photographs by Wolfgang Volz. Text by Werner Spies. Introduction by Herman J. Painitz.

1979 I.C.A., Boston, USA - Laguna Gloria Art Museum, Austin, Texas - Corcoran Gallery of Art, Washington D.C. "Urban Projects." Introduction by Stephen Prokopoff. Text by Pamela Allara and Stephen Prokopoff.

1981 Museum Ludwig, Köln, Germany. Staedel Museum, Frankfurt, Germany. "Urban Projects." Introduction by Karl Ruhrberg and Klaus Gallwitz. Text by Evelyn Weiss and Gerhard Kolberg.

1981 Juda-Rowan Gallery, London, England. "Surrounded Islands, Project for Florida." Photographs by Wolfgang Volz. Text by Anitra Thorhaug.

1981 La Jolla Museum of Contemporary Art, La Jolla, California, USA. Collection on Loan from the Rothschild Bank AG, Zürich. Introduction by Robert McDonald. Text by Jan van der Marck.

1982 Hara Museum of Contemporary Art, Tokyo, Japan."Wrapped Walk Ways." Photographs by Wolfgang Volz. Texts by Toshio Hara, Ellen R. Goheen and Toshio Minemura. Fondation Arc-en-Ciel, Tokyo.

1982 U.A.E. University, Al-Ain, United Arab Emirates. "Environmental Art Works." Photographs by Harry Shunk and Wolfgang Volz. Foreword by Ezzidin Ibrahim.

1984 Satani Gallery, Tokyo, Japan. "The Pont Neuf Wrapped, Project for Paris." Photographs by Wolfgang Volz. Text by Yusuke Nakahara. Interview by Masahiko Yanagi.

1984 Juda-Rowan Gallery, London, England. "Objects, Collages and Drawings. 1958-84."

1984 Architekturmuseum, Basel, Switzerland. "Wrapped Floors," im Architekturmuseum in Basel. Text by Ulrike and Werner Jehle-Schulte. Photographs by Wolfgang Volz.

1986 Satani Gallery, Tokyo, Japan. "Wrapped Reichstag, Project for Berlin." Photographs by Wolfgang Volz. Interview by Masahiko Yanagi.

1986 Galeria Joan Prats, Barcelona, Spain. "Dibuixos i Collages."

1987 Museum of Contemporary Art, Gent, Belgium. "Surrounded Islands," Documentation Exhibition. Photographs by Wolfgang Volz. Text by Werner Spies.

1987 Seibu Museum of Art, Tokyo, Japan. A Collection on Loan from the Rothschild Bank, Zürich. Texts by Torsten Lilja, Yusuke Nakahara, Tokuhiro Nakajima and Akira Moriguchi. Interview by Masahiko Yanagi. Photographs by Wolfgang Volz.

1987 Centre d'Art Nicolas de Staël, Braine-L'Alleud, Belgium. "Dessins, Collages," Photographs. Text by A. M. Hammacher. Interviews by Marcel Daloze and Dominique Verhaegen. Photographs by Wolfgang Volz.

1987 Edition Mönchehaus-Museum Verein zur Förderung Moderne Kunst, Goslar, Germany. Laudation zur Verleihung des Kaiserrings, Goslar, September 26, 1987, Germany. Text by Werner Spies. Photographs by Wolfgang Volz

1988 Satani Gallery, Tokyo, Japan. "The Umbrellas, Joint Project for Japan and USA." Photographs by Wolfgang Volz. Introduction by Ben Yama. Text by Masahiko Yanagi.

1988 Annely Juda Fine Art, London, England. "The Umbrellas, Joint Project for Japan and USA." Photographs by Wolfgang Volz. Interview and text by Masahiko Yanagi.

1988 Taipei Fine Arts Museum, Taipei, Taiwan. "Collection on Loan From the Rothschild Bank AG. Zürich." Preface by Kuang-Nan Huang. Texts by Werner Spies and Joseph Wang. Photographs by Wolfgang Volz.

1989 Guy Pieters Gallery, Knokke-Zoute, Belgium. "The Umbrellas, Joint Project for Japan and USA." Photographs by Wolfgang Volz. Text by Masahiko Yanagi. Picture commentary by Susan Astwood.

1989 Musée d'Art Moderne et d'Art Contemporain, Nice, France. "Selection from the Lilja Collection." Texts by Torsten Lilja, Claude Fournet, Pierre Restany, Werner Spies and Masahiko Yanagi. Photographs by Wolfgang Volz.

1989 Galerie Catherine Issert, St. Paul de Vence, France. "Works: 1965-1988." Text by Raphael Sorin.

1990 The Henie-Onstad Art Centre, Høvikodden, Norway. "Works 1958-89, from the Lilja Collection." Introduction by Torsten Lilja. Text by Per Hovdenakk. Interview by Jan Åman. Photographs by Wolfgang Volz.

1990 Hiroshima City Museum of Contemporary Art - Japan. Hara Museum, ARC, Gunma, Japan – Fukuoka Art Museum, Japan. "Surrounded Islands," Documentation Exhibition. Photographs by Wolfgang Volz. Text by Jonathan Fineberg.

1990 The Art Gallery of New South Wales, Sydney, Australia. "Works from 1958-1990." Foreword by John Kaldor. Texts by Albert Elsen, Toni Bond, Daniel Thomas and Nicholas Baume. Photographs by Wolfgang Volz.

1990 Bogerd Fine Art, Amsterdam, Holland. "Drawings-Multiples."
1990 Gallery Seomi, Seoul, Korea. "Prints and Lithographs.'

1990 Satani Gallery, Tokyo, Japan. "The Umbrellas, Joint Project for Japan and USA." Photographs by Wolfgang Volz. Text by Masahiko Yanagi.

1991 Annely Juda Fine Art, London, England. "Projects Not Realized and Works in Progress." Foreword by Annely Juda and David Juda.
1991 Galeria Joan Prats, Barcelona, Spain. "Obra 1958-1991." Text by Marina Vaizey.

1991 Art Tower Mito, Ibaraki, Japan. "Valley Curtain," Documentation Exhibition. "And The Umbrellas, Joint Project for Japan and USA, Work in Progress." Photographs by Harry Shunk and Wolfgang Volz. Text by Jan van der Marck. Interview by Masahiko Yanagi.

1991 Satani Gallery, Tokyo, Japan."Early Works 1958-64." Text by Masahiko Yanagi and Harriet Irgang.

1992 Gallery Seomi and Gallery Hyundai, Seoul, Korea. Works from the 80's and 90's. Exhibitions curated by Carl Flach. Photographs by Wolfgang Volz.

1992 Marugame Genichiro Inokuma Museum of Contemporary Art, Japan. Valley Curtain, Documentation Exhibition. The Umbrellas, Japan-USA. Photographs by Harry Shunk and Wolfgang Volz. Text by Jan van der Marck. Interview by Masahiko Yanagi.

1993 Art Front Gallery, Hillside Terrace, Tokyo, Japan. "Works from the 80's and 90's." Photographs by Wolfgang Volz. Curated by Carl Flach. Text compiled by Masahiko Yanagi.

1993 "The Reichstag and Urban Projects." Edited by Jacob Baal-Teshuva. Photographs by Wolfgang Volz. Contributions by Tilmann Buddensieg and Wieland Schmied. Interview by Masahiko Yanagi. Chronology by Michael S. Cullen. Prestel-Verlag, München, Germany.

1994 Kunstmuseum, Bonn, Germany. "Christo, The Pont Neuf Wrapped, Paris, 1975- 85." Photographs by Wolfgang Volz. Excerpts from Jeanne-Claude's Agenda. Texts by Volker Adolphs, Bernard de Montgolfier, Dieter Ronte and Constance Sherak.

1995 "Christo and Jeanne-Claude Projects selected from the Lilja Collection." First Edition. Photographs by Wolfgang Volz. Preface by Torsten Lilja. Text by Per Hovdenakk. Azimuth Editions Limited, London, England.

1995 Museum Würth, Künzelsau, Germany. "The Works in the Collection Würth." Texts by Lothar Romain and C. Sylvia Weber. Photographs by Wolfgang Volz. Thorbecke Verlag, Sigmaringen 1995, Germany.

1995 Museum Würth, Künzelsau, Germany. "Wrapped Floors and Stairways and Covered Windows." Photographs by Wolfgang Volz. Edited by C. Sylvia Weber. Texts by Wulf Herzogenrath, Hans Georg Frank, Sibylle Peine, Andreas Sommer, Wolfgang Reiner and Christian Marquart. Thorbecke Verlag, Sigmaringen 1995, Germany.

1995 Annely Juda Fine Art, London, England. "Christo and Jeanne-Claude, Three Works in Progress." Foreword by Annely Juda and David Juda. Photographs by Wolfgang Volz.

1995 Art Front Gallery, Tokyo, Japan. "Wrapped Reichstag, Berlin, and Works in Progress." Photographs by Wolfgang Volz, Sylvia Volz, André Grossmann, Michael Cullen and Yoshitaka Uchida.

1997 Yorkshire Sculpture Park, U.K. "Christo & Jeanne-Claude Sculpture and Projects 1961-96." Preface by Peter Murray. Designed and produced by Claire Glossop.

1997 The Museum of Sketches, Lund, Sweden. "Christo and Jeanne-Claude Projects, works from the Lilja Collection." Introduction by Jan Torsten Ahlstrand. Photographs by Wolfgang Volz.

1998 Galerie Guy Pieters, Belgium. "Christo and Jeanne-Claude, The Gates, Project for Central Park, New York;" and "Over The River, Project for the Arkansas River, Colorado." Photographs by Wolfgang Volz. Designed by Christo. Picture notes by Jeanne-Claude and Jonathan Henery.

1998 Galerie Beyeler, Basel, Switzerland. "Christo and Jeanne-Claude. Exerpts from a text by David Bourdon." Text by Werner Spies.

1999 IBA, Gasometer, Oberhausen, Germany. "Christo and Jeanne-Claude: The Umbrellas, Japan-USA," A documentation Exhibition. "Wrapped Reichstag, Berlin, 1971-95," A Ducumentation Exhibition. "The Wall-13,000 Oil Barrels." Photographs by Wolfgang Volz. Preface by Prof. Karl Ganser. Texts by Marion Taube, David Bourdon and Wolfgang Volz. Edited by Simone Philippi. Benedikt Taschen Verlag GmbH, Köln, Germany.

2000
Annely Juda Fine Art, London, England. Christo and Jeanne-Claude, Black and White.

2001
"Christo e Jeanne-Claude, Progetti Recenti, Progetti Futuri Projects and Realisations for Wrapped Trees, 1966-98; Projects and Realisations with Oil Barrels 1958-82, and !3,000 Oil Barrels, Oberhausen 1999; Two Works in Progress: Over the River and The Gates. "Palazzo Bonoris, Brescia, Italy. Organized by Fondazione Ambrosetti Arte Contemporanea. March 11 to May 21. Catalogue: Texts by Loredana Parmesani, Ettore Camuffo, Marion Taube, Christo and Jeanne-Claude. Photographs by: Wolfgang Volz, Eeva-Inkeri, Jean-Dominique Lajoux, Harry Shunk, Ferdinand Boesch, André Grossmann,

"Christo and Jeanne-Claude: The Art of Gentle Disturbance". Macy Gallery, Teachers College, Columbia University, New York, USA. (Brochure: photographs by Wolfgang Volz, Jean Dominique Lajoux and Harry Shunk.)

"Christo and Jeanne-Claude. Two Works in Progress: Over the River, Project for the Arkansas River, Colorado, and The Gates, Project for Central Park, New York." State University Art Gallery, Kennesaw, Georgia, USA. (Brochure: photographs by Wolfgang Volz.)

"Christo and Jeanne-Claude, The Gates, Project for Central Park New York City.and Over The River, Project for The Arkansas River, Colorado Two works in Progress." Guy Pieters Gallery, Saint Paul de Vence, France. June 16 to July 30. Catalogue: (2 catalogues in a box, edition 2001 "Over the River": picture commentary by Jeanne-Claude and Jonathan Henery, photographs by Wolfgang Volz, Sylvia Volz and Simon Chaput. "The Gates": picture commentary by Jeanne-Claude and Jonathan Henery, photographs by André Grossman and Wolfgang Volz, (In English)

"Christo and Jeanne-Claude, The Gates, Projectfor Central Park New York City.and Over The River, Project for The Arkansas River, Colorado Two works in Progress." Guy Pieters Gallery, Saint Paul de Vence, France. June 16 to July 30. Catalogue: (2 catalogues in a box, edition 2001 "Over the River": picture commentary by Jeanne-Claude and Jonathan Henery, photographs by Wolfgang Volz, Sylvia Volz and Simon Chaput. "The Gates": picture commentary by Jeanne-Claude and Jonathan Henery, photographs by André Grossman and Wolfgang Volz, (In German))

Catalogue: "Early Works 1958-69": Texts by Lawrence Alloway, David Bourdon, Jan van der Marck, photographs by Ferdinand Boesch, Thomas Cugini, André Grossmann Eeva-Inkeri, Jean-Dominique Lajoux, Harry Shunk, Wolfgang Volz, Stefan Wewerka.and many others. Catalogue "Wrapped Reichstag" pictures commentary by David Bourdon, Michael S. Cullen, Christo and Jeanne-Claude, photographs by Wolfgang Volz. Taschen Verlag Publications.

"Christo and Jeanne-Claude, The Pont Neuf Wrapped, Paris, 1975-85, Documentation Exhibition." Fondacao Armando Alvares Penteado, São Paulo, Brazil. Catalogue :texts by Volker Adolphs, Albert Elsen and David Bourdon.. Photographs by Wolfgang Volz

2002
"Christo and Jeanne-Claude in the Vogel Collection." National Gallery of Art, Washington, DC, USA. February 3 to June 23. (Catalogue:Introduction by Earl A. Powell, III; Text and interview by Molly Donovan , photographs by Wolfgang Volz,

2004
"Christo and Jeanne-Claude: On the Way to the Gates." Essay and Interviews by Jonathan Fineberg. Photographs by Wolfgang Volz. Picture Commentary by Jeanne-Claude and Jonathan Henery. Edited by Patricia Fidler; Designed and produced by Ken Wong. Yale University Press, New Haven, CT. and The Metropolitan Museum, New York City.